Monetary Motivation, Performance and Job Satisfaction

A Study at Multicultural For-Profit Institutions of Higher Learning

Dr. Joann Adeogun, PHR

ILEAD Academy, LLC
Davie, Florida. United States of America
www.ileadacademy.com

Joann Adeogun, 2010. *Monetary Motivation, Performance and Job Satisfaction.*

Book Design by: Bahaudin G. Mujtaba
Cover Design by: Cagri Tanyar
Cover Photo by: Paul Sapiano

ISBN-10: 0-9774211-7-1

ISBN-13: 978-0-9774211-6-9

Subject Code & Description
BUS046000 - Business & Economics: Motivational
SEL021000 - Self-Help: Motivational & Inspirational
BUS030000 - Business & Economics: Human Resources & Personnel Management

Printed in the United States of America by ILEAD Academy, LLC. Davie, Florida.

☆ International ☆
ILEAD ACADEMY
Leadership Education and Associate Development Academy

Dedication

This book is dedicated to the memory of my mother Mrs. Venie Delestion who encouraged me to continue to do the right things.

I miss you more than words can say.
Mother's Day – May 10, 2009

TABLE OF CONTENTS

PREFACE

An old saying exists that, "Money makes the world go around." Yet those who are making hundreds of thousands of dollars on the job are not necessarily increasing performance or satisfied with their current employment situation. Several myths exist about the relationship of monetary motivation to job performance and job satisfaction both in for-profit and non-profit higher education institutions. This book explores further through this research study these myths for multicultural for-profit institutions of higher learning. Some of these myths are supported or demystified by the results of this study. My previous experiences as a Director of Compliance, Director of Institutional Effectiveness, trainer, along with instructor at several universities have lead me to conclude that employees want more from the employment relationship than mere compensation in the form of monetary rewards. In the current job market there is a flock to higher education to improve skill-set by students, employees and faculty. This creates a corresponding increase in job performance needs by employers and job satisfaction needs by employees and faculty. "Will monetary motivation unite these needs for all parties involved?"

Monetary Motivation, Performance and Job Satisfaction will provide the following benefits to readers: 1) For the novice working in corporate America – what motivates individuals to do their best and additional insight into money as a motivator; 2) For the more experienced workers – a better understanding of where they fit in within the realm of this research study and hopefully a magnified look at their current level of job performance and job satisfaction. The results of this research can provide better understanding of the variables proposed and can be applied to other organizations, specifically the non-profit industry, which is also undergoing organizational change with respect to student, employee and faculty - attraction, retention and motivation. Practical implications also exist for Human Resource Practitioners as alternative methods of rewards that engage all employees regardless of age, gender, tenure, and educational level are needed to remain competitive in this ever expanding global market. From a strategic perspective, HR Practitioners must play an important role in organizational planning and this book would be a good starting point while formulating incentive plans to retain and attract the organization's human resources. In addition, validation is provided through tables, charts etc. in this book that focus primarily on three areas of concern- monetary motivation, job performance and job satisfaction. This book is relevant to the current times faced by many organizations that must make hard decisions about compensation, rewards and recognition. This material is designed to get the reader to address areas of improvement or confirm areas of excellences within their prospective organizations.

Monetary Motivation, Performance and Job Satisfaction addresses comprehensively the need of organizations to become more competitive while recognizing the need to reward individuals and meet stated organizational objectives in these current turbulent economic times.

ACKNOWLEDGEMENT

Will Monetary Motivation Lead to an Increase in Job Performance and Job Satisfaction? A Study at Multicultural For-Profit Institutions of Higher Learning is a product of my dissertation from Nova Southeastern University, H. Wayne Huizenga School of Business and Entrepreneurship of which this book would not have been possible.

First, nothing is possible without my Lord and Savior. Thank you for all you have done and continue to do in my life.

Second, special thanks go to Dr. Bahaudin G. Mujtaba, Associate Professor of International Management and Human Resources at Nova Southeastern University, H. Wayne Huizenga School of Business and Entrepreneurship for continual mentorship, encouragement and support. Words cannot express my deepest appreciation and gratitude.

Third, I thank each person who has gotten me to this point in my life for your unwavering ability to help me see the bigger picture. Thank you for purchasing and reading this book. If you have additional comments, you can contact me at dradeogun@comcast.net, adeogunassociates@comcast.net or adeogun@nova.edu.

Finally, and most importantly I thank my family, friends and husband Dele Adeogun who supported me without reservation. This book would not have been possible without his sacrifice and love for me. Thank you for teaching me how to let my light shine so that others might see.

```
                ┌─────────────────────────┐
        ╱───────┤                         ├───────╲
      ╱─        │      CHAPTER ONE        │        ─╲
      ╲─        │                         │        ─╱
        ╲───────┤                         ├───────╱
           ╲────┘                         └────╱
```

1 – INTRODUCTION

This chapter introduces this book. It presents a brief background of the problem, purpose of the study, statement of the problem, significance of the study and definition of critical terms. It presents assumptions, limitations, organization of the study, research questions, and working hypotheses.

Background of the Problem

Higher Education is a $650 billion dollar industry (Blumenstyk, 2005b). According to Datamonitor's report of Global Education Services (2005) the higher education sector is highly competitive throughout the globe and colleges and universities compete in terms of courses offered, fee structure, time needed to earn degrees, cost of program and reliability and experience of their faculty.

The $15.4 billion for-profit higher education industry is growing leaps and bound both politically and financially (Blumenstyk, 2005a). According to Blumenstyk this growth is due to the friendly legislative environment, increased enrollments, profits and opportunity for further expansion and profitability. Another area of growth in the for-profit higher education industry is the changing demand of students (Blumenstyk, 2005b). For-profit higher learning institutions according to Eduventures account for 8 % of the 20 million students enrolled, 2.4 % of the 400,000 students at degree granting institutions and one-third of online enrollments (Blumenstyk, 2005a). Jerry Herman of Stifel Nicolaus Education Research states that enrollment at proprietary schools nationwide has been growing 25-30 % a year (Stockman, 2006). Enrollment at the nation's 2,700 for-profit career colleges now tops 2.1 million and is growing by 17 % annually since 2003-2004 (Blumenstyk, 2007b). Table 1 represents the competitive landscape of four of the largest publicly traded for-profit higher education companies.

Table 1 - For-Profit Education Industry Competitive Landscape 2006

Key Numbers	Apollo Group	1 Year Growth	Career Edu.	1 Year Growth	DeVry	1 Year Growth	ITT Edu.	1 Year Growth
Annual Sales -$mil.	2,4775	10.0%	1,785.6	(12.2%)	843.3	7.9	757.8	10.1%
Employees	36,416	11.5%	16,740	2.6%	4,800	(15.8%)	6,200	3.3%
Market Cap ($mil.)	9,616.8	_____	2,563.0	_____	2,545.5	_____	4,390	_____
Net Income ($mil.)	_____	(6.7%)	_____	(80.1%)	_____	50.8%	_____	8.0%

Source: Hoover's (2007), $mil=Million

With all the growth that the for-profit education industry is experiencing, recent developments signal that challenges exist (Blumenstyk, 2007a; Blumenstyk, 2007c; Woods, 2006).

Apollo Group is accused of backdating to award options and subsequently several shareholders have sued the company.

Career Education's American InterContinental University was placed on probationary status for another year in December 2006 by the Southern Association of Colleges and Schools.

DeVry University announced a voluntary separation plan of employees who work at larger campus site in March 2007.

The FBI raided 10 campuses of ITT Educational Services Group in pursue of claims of recruitment violation in February 2004.

The for-profit higher learning industry is highly competitive and both current and would be employees expect competitive salaries. In agreement, Tang (2006) states to attract, retain, and motivate employees around the world an understanding is needed of the importance of money.

The College and University Professional Association for Human Resource (2006) in its Think Tank Report on the Future of Higher Education writes the following regarding the external threats faced by higher education:

> "Low salaries, high expectations and inflexible practices make academic careers increasingly unappealing. This is especially true for women and Ph.D.s in the disciplines of science and engineering."

The for-profit education industry appears to spend less on salaries for faculty members and facilities than the nonprofit sector according to Samuel Woods a lecturer at Stanford University (Blumenstyk, 2006a). One way the for-profit education industry has held down the cost of instruction is by redefining the role of faculty who teach from a curriculum, as a result faculty members are paid lower salaries than at traditional colleges where faculty members play a greater role in designing and creating courses (Blumenstyk, 2006a). According to Samuel Woods the for-profit colleges have found a way to hire relatively low corps of faculty to attract students (Blumenstyk, 2006a).

Harris Miller president of The Career College Association states in his Economic-Impact Study that proprietary colleges employ approximately 137,041 full-time staff and faculty and pay about $8 billion in salaries (Blumenstyk, 2007b).

For-profit institutions show no signs of decreasing in market share, but what types of incentives are they willing to offer to motivate performance and satisfaction of individuals who are supporting and generating the aforementioned revenue growth?

Given the success of for-profit institutions and the existing literature on monetary motivation, it is therefore essential that an understanding of the relationship between monetary motivation and increased job performance and job satisfaction at multicultural for-profit institutions of higher learning is examined.

Purpose of the Study

An organization's reward system is an important factor that can potentially lead to an increase in job performance and job satisfaction of workers. Several studies show money as a motivational tool to enhance performance levels and influence satisfaction. However, no such research yet focuses on the for-profit industry. Therefore, the major purpose of this study is to determine if monetary motivation leads to an increase in job performance and job satisfaction at multicultural for-profit institutions of higher learning.

Statement of the Problem

The for-profit industry is going through a transformation that results both in voluntary and involuntary turnover of employees and students at higher education institutions. Money is perceived as a means to recruit, select and retain valued members of an organization; however, it is not known if increased job performance and job satisfaction are the by-products of such initiatives in multicultural for-profit institutions of higher learning. Higher pay levels signal to individuals that they matter to their organization. Therefore, the research model used in this study has been developed to determine if increased job performance and job satisfaction is a result of monetary motivation. Three instruments are used to determine the impact monetary motivation has on increased job performance and job satisfaction: (a). Money Ethics Scale (MES), (b). Job Involvement Scale (JIS), and (c). Minnesota Satisfaction Questionnaire (MSQ).

Significance of the Study

The study is significant in steering for-profit institutions toward an understanding of what motivates individuals to increase job performance and job satisfaction. Numerous researchers have examined compensation, job performance and job satisfaction in many types of organizations. However, this study is unique as it investigates money attitudes as a motivational tool to increase job performance and job satisfaction at multicultural for-profit institutions of higher learning.

This study is therefore important in providing empirical evidence for the for-profit higher learning industry. All participants in this proposed study are employees and students at for-profit institutions of higher learning.

Definition of Critical Terms

The following definitions are considered critical terms for this study and are included for clarification:

Money. According to Furnham and Argyle (1998) money is a medium of exchange and has objective functions. It can be used to acquire goods and services and as a unit of account. Money is also a store of value and a standard of deferred payment. The most obvious way that money is used in the employee-organization relationship is that companies pay employees in exchange for their labor (Mitchell & Mickel, 1999).

Motivation. Vroom (1964) defined motivation as processes governed by personal choices as an alternate to other activities. Vroom's Expectancy Theory postulates that motivation is determined by three factors: (1) the perception that effort will result in success; (2) the perception that a successful performance will lead to a valued outcome - a reward of some kind; (3) and that personal satisfaction will be derived from the outcome.

Job Performance. Job performance is defined for the purpose of this study as the action, behaviors and outcomes engaged in by employees that are linked and contribute to organizational goals (Viswesvaran & Ones, 2000).

Job Satisfaction. Morse (1953) and Porter (1962) view satisfaction as the result that job needs are being fulfilled. Flanagan, Strauss and Ulman (1974) define job satisfaction as the pleasure an individual derives from his or her work. Factors that affect job satisfaction include pay, working hours, complexity and difficulty of job, promotion prospects and personal relationships with coworkers.

Multicultural. Multicultural is defined for the purpose of this study as a diverse population that includes several cultures and or ethnic groups (Canen & Canen, 2001).

For-Profit Institution. For the purpose of this research for-profit institutions are established and operate for the sole purpose of making a profit (Kinser & Levy, 2005).

Assumptions

The researcher has made several assumptions regarding this study. First, the subjects completing the survey will take adequate time to respond honestly and truthfully. Second, participants will have access to a computer and some level of computer competency. Third, the data collection method will be appropriate for the sample population being studied. Fourth, the Money Ethics Scale (MES) by Tang (1992), Job Involvement Scale (JIS) by Lodahl and Kejner (1965) and Cammann, Fichman, Jenkins and Klesh (1979) and the Minnesota Satisfaction Questionnaire by

Weiss, Dawis, England and Lofquist (1967) are appropriate measurement tools for the for-profit industry. Last, assumptions are made by the researcher that the responses will be of use in making generalities regarding the relationship between monetary motivation, job performance and job satisfaction.

Limitation of the Study

Several limitations exist for this study. First, this study takes place in the for-profit higher learning industry and is limited to employees and students. Second, survey participants may not understand the complete scope of the research and their responses may not reflect their current job situation in its entirety. Third, the sample of the study may not adequately represent the for-profit industry in general. Fourth, the size of the institutions selected in the proposed study may influence results. Last, both advantages and disadvantages of the survey techniques are recognized.

Organization of the Study

This book is composed of five chapters. Chapter one introduces the following sections: a). background of the problem, b). purpose of the study, c). statement of the problem, d). significance of the study, e). definitions of critical terms, f). assumptions, g). limitations and h). research questions and working hypotheses.

Chapter two presents the literature review and describes the following sections: a). Monetary Motivation (Age, Gender Wage Gap, Tenure, Educational Level, Equity Theory, Extrinsic Rewards, Pay Satisfaction and Organizational Worth), b). Job Performance (Performance Levels), and c). Job Satisfaction (Environmental Influences).

Chapter three introduces the methodology and includes: a). corresponding population and sample, b). research variables and relationship of variables, c). operational definitions, d). survey instruments, e). reliability and validity, f). data collection procedure, g). research questions with their respective hypotheses, h). data analysis and strategy and i). limitations of the study.

Chapter four analyzes the data collected and presents the findings of the study.

Chapter five provides a summation of the research study findings in retrospect of monetary motivation at for-profit institutions, limitations of this study and recommendations for future research.

Research Questions

The major purpose of this study is to determine if monetary motivation (money attitudes) affects increased job performance and job satisfaction at multicultural for-profit institutions of higher learning. The following research questions guide the hypotheses of this study:

- **Q1**. Is monetary motivation related to job performance at multicultural for-profit institutions of higher learning?
- **Q2**. Is monetary motivation related to job satisfaction at multicultural for-profit institutions of higher learning?

Working Hypotheses

The 10 research hypotheses derived from the research questions to test the relationship between monetary motivation (money attitudes) and increased job performance and job satisfaction are as follows:

- **H01**: The effects of monetary motivation on job performance will decrease or have no effect with age at multicultural for-profit institutions of higher learning.
- **H1A**: The effects of monetary motivation on job performance will increase or have no effect with age at multicultural for-profit institutions of higher learning.
- **H02**: The effects of monetary motivation on job satisfaction will decrease or have no effect with age at multicultural for-profit institutions of higher learning.
- **H2A**: The effects of monetary motivation on job satisfaction will increase or have no effect with age at multicultural for-profit institutions of higher learning.
- **H03**: The effects of monetary motivation on job performance will be higher for females than males at multicultural for-profit institutions of higher learning.
- **H3A**: The effects of monetary motivation on job performance will be lower for females than males at multicultural for-profit institutions of higher learning.
- **H04**: The effects of monetary motivation on job satisfaction will be higher for males than females at multicultural for-profit institutions of higher learning.
- **H4A**: The effects of monetary motivation on job satisfaction will be lower for males than females at multicultural for-profit institutions of higher learning.
- **H05**: The effects of monetary motivation on job performance will increase with tenure at multicultural for-profit institutions of higher learning.
- **H5A**: The effects of monetary motivation on job performance will decrease with tenure at multicultural for-profit institutions of higher learning.
- **H06**: The effects of monetary motivation on job satisfaction will increase with tenure at multicultural for-profit institutions of higher learning.
- **H6A**: The effects of monetary motivation on job satisfaction will decrease with tenure at multicultural for-profit institutions of higher learning.

- **H07**: The effects of monetary motivation on job performance will increase with educational level of the employee at multicultural for-profit institutions of higher learning.
- **H7A**: The effects of monetary motivation on job performance will decrease with educational level of the employee at multicultural for-profit institutions of higher learning.
- **H08**: The effects of monetary motivation on job satisfaction will increase with educational level at multicultural for-profit institutions of higher learning.
- **H8A**: The effects of monetary motivation on job satisfaction will decrease with educational level at multicultural for-profit institutions of higher learning.
- **H09**: The effects of monetary motivation on job performance will increase at multicultural for-profit institutions of higher learning.
- **H9A**: The effects of monetary motivation on job performance will decrease at multicultural for-profit institutions of higher learning.
- **H10**: The effects of monetary motivation on job satisfaction will increase at multicultural for-profit institutions of higher learning.
- **H10A**: The effects of monetary motivation on job satisfaction will decrease at multicultural for-profit institutions of higher learning.

Summary

For-profit institutions are in the business to make a profit; however, productivity may be in jeopardy if employees are not motivated or satisfied with incentives. To face this ever changing competitive environment of the for-profit higher learning industry employers are tasked with finding creative ways to increase both job performance and job satisfaction. The purpose of this book is to determine if monetary motivation results in increased job performance and job satisfaction at multicultural for-profit institutions of higher learning.

Based on the proposed research hypotheses, this study examines the influence of monetary motivation on job performance and job satisfaction at multicultural for-profit institutions of higher learning. The next chapter describes monetary motivation, job performance and job satisfaction. Specifically, it discusses the relationships of monetary motivation, job performance and job satisfaction.

CHAPTER TWO

II - LITERATURE REVIEW

The purpose of this study is to examine the relationship between monetary motivation (money attitudes) and both job performance and job satisfaction at multicultural for-profit institutions of higher learning. This chapter presents a review of the literature for this study in the following order: monetary motivation (money attitudes), job performance and job satisfaction.

Earlier researchers in the area of motivation, compensation, work, job performance, job satisfaction and organizational effectiveness are of the opinion that employers must have a better understanding of what employees want and need in the employment relationship (Herzberg, Mausner & Snyderman, 1959; Lawler, 1971; Likert, 1967; Roethlisberger, Dickson & Wright, 1956; Vroom, 1964). In order for employees to feel a high degree of interest in their job and obtain satisfaction the employee must be motivated and productive (Collins, 1982). According to Kovach (1987) managers must create a climate in which most employees "…will find it personally rewarding to motivate themselves and in the process contribute to the company's attainment of objectives." Yet another supporter states that surprise should be removed from the workplace in order to motivate employees. This can be accomplished by advising employees of what is expected of them, how they will be measured, and when they will be measured (Kauffman, 1987).

An additional area of concern for employees is meeting their personal objectives. Renier (1983) states that no business can reach its productivity objectives unless that business also provides a way for employees to reach their personal objectives. According to Babcock (2005) understanding what matters to employees is not an incidental undertaking as companies can maximize by investing in human capital. Young (1997) states that employment establishes a relationship of employer and employee. This research examines the extent to which monetary motivation by the employer as assessed by the employee is related to increased performance and satisfaction. The literature review is divided into three main sections. The first section discusses monetary motivation theory as manifested by extrinsic rewards (and its effect on employees) and pay satisfaction theory and its importance to workers; the second section reviews the literature on job performance; then follows a section that reviews the literature on job satisfaction. Figure 1 depicts the relationships among the variables.

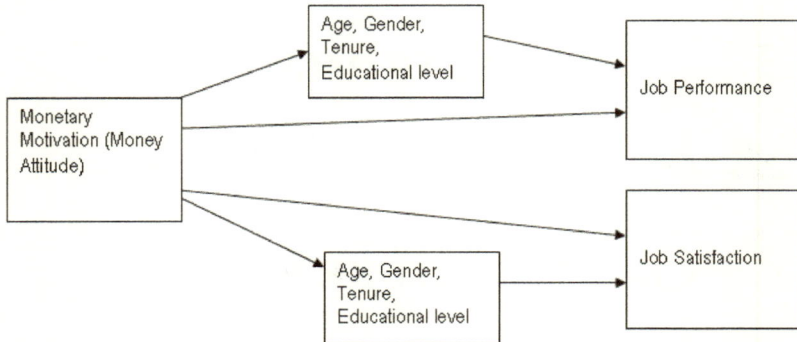

Figure 1- The Relationship between Monetary Motivation (Money Attitudes), increased Job Performance and Job Satisfaction

Monetary Motivation

This first section of the literature reviews previous research on monetary motivation and includes several related topics: Studies on definitions and measures of motivation to work, age, tenure, educational level, gender, equity theory, extrinsic rewards, pay satisfaction and organizational worth.

Regardless of whether employees view money as a major motivator or as a component of overall motivation, employees are constantly comparing themselves to others and will continue to do so. Gender differences influence individual equity perceptions of fair wages and what is considered an equitable or acceptable reward system. Satisfaction with ones pay has a direct affect on if the employee feels valued and a sense of organizational worth. The underlying question of this research is "How does each of these variables relate to higher education?"

Motivation has been defined by many researchers over the years; however, Merriam-Webster defines motivation as the act or process of motivating: the condition of being motivated: a motivating force, stimulus, or influence: incentive or drive (Merriam-Webster, 2006). Vroom (1964) played an instrumental role in getting managers and others to think about what motivates employees to work. His definition of motivation included processes governed by personal choices as an alternate to other activities. Vroom believed that the majority of individuals worked for reasons that had nothing to do with money. Individuals want to obtain skills, acceptance, respect and the opportunity to contribute to society and money was just a necessary part of the work-motivation relationship (Vroom, 1964).

According to Ross and Zander (1957) in order to attract and retain employee in an organization his or her needs must first be satisfied. Those needs would include a competitive salary and other company perks. Millman (2007) writes that faculty salaries beat inflation for the first time in 3 years due in part to top university endowments that attract top faculty members offering higher salaries, development opportunities, newer facilities and cutting edge technology.

Many have said that, "Money makes the world go round." Yet those who are making hundreds of thousands of dollars on the job are not necessarily increasing performance or satisfied with their current employment. What is money anyway?

According to Furnham and Argyle (1998) money is a medium of exchange and has objective functions. It can be used to acquire goods and services and as a unit of account. Money is also a store of value and a standard of deferred payment. The most obvious way that money is used in the employee-organization relationship is that companies pay employees in exchange for their labor (Mitchell & Mickel, 1999). According to Milkovich and Newman (1993) money is used by organization as an attraction, motivation and retention tool; they use money to reward and recognize, and they withhold it as punishment. Symbolically, money is often associated with four of the most important symbolic goods humans strive for: (1) achievement and recognition, (2) status and respect, (3) freedom and control, and (4) power, therefore, it is an aspect of motivation because of what it stands for. It is frequently used to recognize accomplishments (Kirkcaldy & Furnham, 1993; Tang, 1992) and often engenders status and respect from others (Goldberg & Lewis, 1978). Money can provide the luxury of time, autonomy, and freedom (Goldberg & Lewis, 1978; Parsons 1967) as well as power and access to resources.

How important is money to the employee and can it be used by the employer as a motivator to benefit the organization's bottom line? Should employees compare themselves to others in the organization and if they do, will the comparison result in increased performance and job satisfaction or the opposite? How important is the gender of the compared other in the monetary motivation process? Is money the reward system that motivates employees to work harder? What constitutes pay satisfaction for the employee and does the pay from the employer determine organizational worth? The answers to these questions will be addressed in the literature that follows.

In pure economic terms, monetary compensation is viewed as fundamental to the exchange relationship between employers and employees (Singh, Fujita & Norton, 2004). In general, there appears to be a consistent (but incorrect) message to practitioners that pay is not a very effective motivator – a message that, if believed, could cause practitioners to underestimate seriously the motivational potential of a well-designed compensation system (Rynes, Gerhart & Minette, 2004). Truby (2003) conducted a study of PhD. colleagues to better understand the "anecdotes of frustration" of university lecturers and concluded that money, time, security and status were at the forefront. In Hemmasi, Graf and Lust (1992) study of 518 public university faculties it was determined that members of social science, humanities or education disciplines were less satisfied with compensation. The same study concluded that those faculty members who view the job as overly demanding were less satisfied with their compensation and indirect benefits. Comm and Mathaisel

(2003) studied faculty members at a private college to better understand issues of teaching load, workload and compensation. The researchers concluded that 59 % of faculty felt teaching load had increased, 72 % felt workload had increased and 51 % of faculty did not believe they were compensated fairly.

Rynes et al. (2004) agreed that managers and employees should exam the systematic underestimation of the importance of pay. Rynes et al. (2004) argue that in the case of pay, people are likely to understate its importance either because they misjudge how employees might react to an offer of a higher paying job. Due to social norms people view money as a less noble source of motivation than factors such as challenging work or work that makes a contribution to society (Rynes et al, 2004). Moreover, in emphasizing the importance of pay as a motivator, we are not saying that pay is the only important motivator (Rynes et al, 2004).

So, if money is not the only important motivator why do people go to work day after day? According to Vroom (1995) we are much more likely to wonder why people climb mountains or commit suicide than to question the motivational basis of their work. Russell (1930) argued that the purpose of work is essential for happiness. To Russell (1930), even the dullest of work is less dissatisfying than idleness-it fills many hours of the day for employees; it provides a chance for success and an opportunity to excel. Gini (2000) states that because work consumes so much of our lives, we must reinvent or, perhaps more accurately, at least recapture three primary tenets with regard to work and the person: 1). Adult fulfillment, 2). Help to produce better people and life, 3). Seen as a fundamental part of our humanity (p. 3). Herzberg (1968) states that the only way that employees can be motivated is to give them challenging work with assumed responsibility. Kovack (1987) points out that a company would be in a better position to stimulate employees to perform well, if that company knew what drove employees to work.

Employees must be asked on a regular basis what sparks and sustains their desire to work. Their responses may lead the employer to redesign jobs, increase pay, change the working environment, or give more credit for work done. The key, however, is that managers avoid the assumption that what motivates them also motivates their employees as well (Wessler, 1984).

Money is not everything. Many would be happy with more time off or more job security than more money (Furnham, 2005). Piamonte (1979) states that earlier researchers, such as, Maslow, Herzberg and others introduced the idea that money is not the only motivator. However, with this introduction of various other motivators; monetary rewards moved down on the list or off the list altogether in importance.

Age

Researchers in the area of age and job performance have concluded that no relationship exists (McEvoy & Cascio, 1989; Waldman & Avolio, 1986). In fact, Chu, Chan, Snape and Redman (2001) write that older workers are not any less productive than his or her younger counterparts. The Age Discrimination in Employment Act (ADE) provides equal employment opportunity on the basis of age and was amended in 1986 to specify protection for those 40 and over unless the employer can show that age is Bona Fide Occupational Qualification (Cascio & Aguinis, 2005).

According to Snyder and Brandon (1983) to motivate older workers the supervisors and managers must be educated to value workers as valuable resources. Kauffman (1987) writes that older workers are motivated by intrinsic rewards such as a pat on the back. According to Bourne (1982) pay and promotions appear to be less important for older workers. Saks and Waldman (1998) found in their study a negative relationship between age, evaluations of technical and overall job performance. These researchers concluded that little differences exist between younger and older workers in entry level jobs. Tang (1992) writes in his study that money attitudes of young adults are influenced by their age – money seen as evil. Tu, Plaisent, Bernard and Maguiraga (2005) conducted a study of 194 Taiwanese and 211 Chinese faculty regarding comparative age differences on job satisfaction at public and private colleges and universities. The result of the study found that both the Taiwanese and Chinese faculty found the most important factor of job satisfaction to be interaction with colleagues. For Taiwanese faculty age 41-50 financial rewards and workload are strategies that meet job satisfaction.

Gender

Empirical data has shown that women earn 72% of what men earn for essentially the same job with the identical qualification, skills and experience (AFL-CIO, 2006). Benjamin (2001) stated in Academe – The Annual Report on the Economic Status of the Profession 2000-2001 that:

> "The disparity between male and female salaries persists and, in some respects, continues to widen. Men earn 6.5 % more than women in public institutions, 5.9 % more in independent institutions, and 10 % more in research institutions."

According to Hinrichs (1969) individuals' perceptions of equitable pay may be significantly affected by two major demographic variables; (a) current pay level, and (b) earning potential (education, age, sex). Alkadry and Tower (2006) in there study "Unequal Pay: The Role of Gender" found that several reasons contributed to differences in women and men salaries in similar positions and in the same field of work. Gender was one of the reasons. Traditionally, the pay differences between men and women have been attributed to women in limited higher paying upper positions within organizations (Alkadry & Tower, 2006). However, the pay gap when a discussion of pay equity takes place maybe attributed to a women's tenure, educational differences and or work experiences compared to men (Alkadry & Tower, 2006).

Laboratory studies found that the sex of a comparison person influences individuals' perceptions of that comparison person's inputs (Taynor & Deaux, 1973, 1975). Furthermore, an individual's sex may influence that individual's equity perception (Wahba, 1971). The literature is long and consistent in reporting that women do not have significantly higher levels of dissatisfaction with pay even though the existence of a wage gap between men and women is widely known (Crosby 1976; Sauser & York, 1978; Smith, Kendall & Hulin, 1969). Tang and Talpade (1999) stated that males tend to have higher satisfaction with pay than females, whereas females tend to have higher satisfaction with coworkers than males. Additionally, these results seem to support previous findings regarding the importance of employees' needs. More specifically, men may value money more highly than females. Further, money (pay) may satisfy esteem needs that are important to men, whereas coworker may satisfy social needs that are important to women (Tang & Talpade, 1999). Balkin and Gomez-Mejia (2002) report that women seek other women as pay references to lessen the frustration comparison that would be the case when making cross-gender pay comparisons. By choosing same gender pay references, women are more likely to sustain perceptions of pay equity rather than trying to achieve pay parity with males (Balkin & Gomez-Mejia, 2002). According to Bender, Donohue and Heyward (2005) the characteristics associated with women's jobs may appeal to them adequately to overcome the satisfaction lost of lower earnings.

Okpara, Squillace and Erondu (2004) research on gender difference and job satisfaction reported that female academics were less satisfied with their work overall, possibly because they are conscious of the salary gap. Moreover, they see the gap as unfair and attribute its existence, along with the glass ceiling and other issues in higher education, to discrimination (Okpara et al., 2004). A prime example is a lawsuit filed by 8 professors at Penn State alleging gender bias in pay and pension (Gravois, 2007). The women are requesting back pay, retirement benefits and better pay in the further (Gravois, 2007). Researchers recommended that universities break the glass ceiling by paying both sexes comparable salaries for comparable work responsibilities thus increasing satisfaction, retention, performance, and productivity while reducing turnover and absenteeism (Okpara et al., 2004). Experts believe that between 10 and 30 % of the wage gap between women and men is attributable to wage discrimination (SHRM Workplace Trend Program, 2006). According to the SHRM Workplace Trend Program (2006) the wage differentials between women and men could have long-term affect on income levels, work patterns and labor participation rates for both genders.

According to Wasley (2007) the report from the American Association of University Women Education Foundation states that the gap between men and women salaries widens overtime even though women makeup the majority of college students. The report goes further to state that one year after graduation women earn 80 % of her male counterpart and 69 % 10 years later (Wasley, 2007). The inequities in pay are due to choices of college attended and college major (Wasley, 2007).

A study published in the September 2006 issue of the Harvard Business Review states that a steady support has grown over the last 40 years for the idea of women in senior management positions from 35 % to 88 %, however a gap still exist in equity and bias attitudes (Hastings, 2007).

Tang, Tang and Homaifar (2006) argue that women are taking on greater responsibility in the workplace and additional roles in money matter; thus money importance maybe enhancing their love of money.

Tenure

According to the American Association of University Professors the purpose of tenure is to ensure academic freedom (teach, research etc.) without the fear of censure or job loss (Williams & Ceci, 2007). Brand (1999) states that tenure is indispensable and has a vital role to play in our higher education system. The primary purpose of tenure is to assess job performance (Barron, 2003). Shapiro (2001) writes that the career path of tenure faculty is relatively unmarked by changes in job description or title. In fact, Barron (2003) states that tenure comes with little or no ceremony, with the exception of possibly a party.

In the last two decades, the increase in the number of faculty employed in contingent positions (non-tenure part or full-time) probably represents the single most significant development in higher education (Curtis, 2005). The higher education's tenure system increases institutional flexibility and reduces labor cost by hiring faculty outside the tenure system (Monk, 2007). Monk states that not only are contingent faculty (non-tenure part and full-time) paid less than traditional tenure-track faculty but they are also paid less per class section and per hour. A study by the Center for the Education of Women (August, Hollenshead, Miller & Waltman, 2006) in their survey report *Non Tenure Track Faculty: The Landscape at U.S. Institutions of Higher Education* found that many of the institutions do not recognize performance or merit in the adjustments for compensation of non-tenure track faculty. The survey further revealed that half of non-tenure track faculties are not rewarded monetarily for job performance (August, Hollenshead, Miller & Waltman, 2006). Many scholars have recommended a reduction in non-tenure faculty and argue that part and full-time non-tenure faculty are less committed to students (Wilson, 1998). Ehrenberg and Zhang (2005) conducted a study using panel data to address the usage of full and part-time non-tenured faculty on undergraduate students' graduation rates. The study concluded that the growth in non-tenure (part and full-time) faculty adversely affects enrollment of undergraduate students and reduced five and six year graduation rates at four-year colleges and universities. In contrast, Wilson (1998) writes that for some the tenure track holds little appeal as some non-tenure faculty welcome flexibility.

Bedeian, Ferris and Kacmar (1992) conducted a study of 821 nonacademic employees at a university in the southeastern United States to determine the relationship between age, tenure and job satisfaction. The result of the study concluded that tenure is a better predictor of job satisfaction than chronological age. A survey conducted by the Harvard University's Graduate School of Education of 4,500 tenure-track faculty members at 51 colleges and university concluded that job satisfaction as it relates to compensation, workload and tenure was not as important as departmental climate, culture and how well they got along with colleagues (Fogg, 2006).

According to Leslie (1998) approximately 30% of colleges and universities and one-third of community colleges have no tenure system in place. Vancouver Community College in British Columbia has found a way solve the issue of less paid non-tenure faculty by first changing the status from full or part-time tenure and non-tenure to regular or term classification paid on a pro rata basis in line with full-time tenured faculty (Longmate & Cosco, 2002).

Educational Level

According to Wise (1975) a college education enhances productivity of college graduates. Truxillo, Bennett and Collins (1998) state that education may be useful as a predictor of performance but also play a role in employee development. Loury (1997) writes that the relationship between educational performance, productivity and earning may not be the same at all schooling levels. McEwen (1998) in his study of 82 alumni of a midwestern state university employed as managers found the type of college degree had no significant effect on communication skills of managers; however, the level of college degree affects communication only in public speaking abilities. Allen and Velden (2001) in their study found that job satisfaction is influenced by wages, self-employed are more satisfied and skill mismatch has a strong influence on job satisfaction. Shauman (2006) writes that sex differences in college major could be due to sex segregation as men are more like to choose college majors that are strongly linked to occupations in the labor market (e.g. science, engineering) or sex differences could be due to employment patterns within college major occupation.

According to Rainey (2006) a decline exists in degrees obtained in science, technology, engineering and mathematics despite the increase in college enrollment. The solution is to increase outreach efforts from kindergarten-12th grade with special emphasize on female and minority students and mentorship programs that target these areas (Rainey, 2006). Hickok (2006) writes that higher education needs a transformation in the way it "schools" students and faculty. A movement towards educational entrepreneurship of fresh ideas, faces and true leadership in schools and colleges is needed (Hickok, 2006).

Higher education attainment will ultimately lead to wage moderation due in part to larger numbers of qualified applicants (Gray & Chapman, 1999).

Equity Theory

Equity theory is a social comparison theory that proposes that employees compare their inputs to outcome ratio in the workplace to those of others. Inputs are what the employee brings to the workplace, such as education, experience and the work itself. Outcomes are mostly monetary and can include fringe benefits or other indirect compensation that one gets out of the job. Whenever the employee feels inequity in the employment relationship, he or she will take steps to even out the playing field. Comparing inputs to outcomes results in one of three feelings: (1) "over-reward," when outcomes exceed inputs; (2) "equitable reward," when inputs equal outcomes; (3) "under-reward," when inputs exceed outcomes (Huseman & Hatfield, 1990).

In agreement, Terpstra and Honoree (2005) state that perceived inequity will lead to tension and that tension will motivate the individual to reduce the inequity. Researchers suggest that feeling undercompensated or inequitably treated can lead to numerous negative behaviors, such as turnover (Summers & Hendrix, 1991), theft (Greenberg, 1990), and lower product quality (Cowherd & Levine, 1992). According to McAfee and Glassman (2005) some employees may respond to inequity by leaving the organization at a time of worker shortages or reduce or minimize work level. Goltz (2005) conducted a study to address attempts to restore equity of women within American universities. The result of the study concluded that women use both informal and formal attempts to restore inequity; however, their concerns are often met with non-response, denial, delay and retaliation. According to Kerber (2005) gender inequities in academia still exist even though women are educated, take on more responsibility and are a larger portion of the workforce. Flexibility is needed to make the academic workplace more equitable for women (Kerber, 2005). In agreement, Wilson (2004) states that gender inequity exist for women at major research universities due to slower advancement to tenure track, compensation and job dissatisfaction.

Overpayment researchers (Garland, 1973; Greenberg & Leventhal, 1976) found that adults believe overpayment to be an effective means of improving the performance of others. According to McDowell, Boyd and Bowler (2007) overrewarded individuals may feel indebted to the organization and increase contributions to achieve an equitable situation. Organizational consequences of overreward maybe both positive and negative depended on the dispositional characteristic of the employee (McDowell et al, 2007). Overreward may result in higher performance levels to accomplish equity, but at a sacrifice of low job satisfaction and increased stress (McDowell et al, 2007).

Extrinsic Rewards

This section reviews previous research on extrinsic rewards and its effects on employees and includes several related topics: Studies on organizational reward systems, incentive plans, financial stress and the negative impact of rewards.

Money and verbal reinforcement are extrinsic rewards which are mediated outside the person, whereas intrinsic rewards are mediated within the person (Deci, 1972). According to Deci (1972) a person is intrinsically motivated if there is no apparent reward to perform an activity except the activity or feeling resulting from the activity. Chen, Gupta and Hoshower (2006) in their study of 320 faculty members at 10 midwestern business schools investigated the impact of 13 rewards (extrinsic and intrinsic) from research on faculty motivation. It was determined that faculty with high extrinsic and intrinsic motivation published more articles. The same study concluded that untenured faculties are more motivated by extrinsic rewards and tenured faculties are more motivated by intrinsic rewards.

According to Buhler (1989) an organization's reward system serves the organization in both internal and external ways. The internal benefits include increased job performance, decreased absenteeism and decreased turnover. A good reward system motivates people to work harder. Increased productivity, therefore; saves the organization money in terms of both overtime pay and the cost of selecting and hiring additional employees. Kratz and Mets (2005) in their research of incentive plans to assess faculty satisfaction found that 80 % of the faculty did not understand how incentives were determined, 40 % did not feel the incentive plan played a role in increased productivity and 35 % agreed they were satisfied with the current incentive plan.

However, according to Kreps (1997) extrinsic incentives can be counterproductive, as it can destroy intrinsic motivation of the worker. The result is lesser levels of effort and net profit lost for the employer. This is not to say that intrinsic motivation is always superior to extrinsic incentives.

Peiperl and Jones (2001) state that although individuals tend to work for a variety of reasons and expect a number of extrinsic rewards from working, the most visible and easily quantifiable return from the individual's work are usually financial. Additional surveys and research support Peiperl and Jones' view of finance as the link to why individuals work. According to a Los Angeles Times survey, 27% of Americans characterize their personal finances as shaky and 40% report having difficulty making installment loans, car payments or insurance premiums. Other researchers indicate that between 15% and 20% of U.S. employees experience financial stress to such a degree that it interferes with their productivity in the workplace (Kim & Garman, 2004). In agreement, Lenhart and Birschel (2006) state that frequent financial distress of workers can lead to lost sleep, distraction at work, increase in absenteeism, healthcare cost, and ultimately lost productivity. In order to determine the relationship between financial stress and work outcome variables, questionnaires were mailed to white-collar employees of an insurance company with worksites located in three Midwestern states. The questionnaire results indicate that the employees were the least likely to be productive and the most likely to be absent from work. Therefore, financial stress appears to have a negative impact on employees and companies (Lenhart and Birschel, 2006). In order to help employees better manage their finances and reduce overall financial stress, employers should consider providing employee access to financial education, advice and counseling (Kim & Garman, 2004). Employers who sponsor such programs can expect at least 300% of the program's cost as a potential return according to The National Institute of Personal Finance Employee Education (Lenhart & Birschel, 2006).

According to Benabou and Tirole (2003) the potential negative impact of rewards should be viewed from that of the provider to determine if private information is known about the agent's talent. A given individual's reaction to a specific reward distribution will be affected by his or her place in that distribution, by whether or not the distribution is perceived as being equitable or fair, by whether or not the person has information about the distribution and his or her place in it, and finally, by the person's relationship and commitment to the organization (Pfeffer & Langton, 1993). An immediate result of a good extrinsic reward system is satisfaction with pay.

Pay Satisfaction

This section discusses pay satisfaction and its importance for workers and includes several related topics: Studies on comparative salary, pay dissatisfaction and performance outcomes.

According to Sweeney and McFarlin (2005) one of the most important rewards from working is pay. Pay satisfaction beyond pay level is determined by the employee's sense of fairness due in part to pay comparison (Sweeney & McFarlin, 2005).

The amount of salary and pay satisfaction of workers has a direct positive correlation (Greenberg, 1987). One of the most widely used models in pay satisfaction was proposed by Lawler (1971, 1981). He proposes that satisfaction with one's pay is a result of what the employee expects to receive as opposed to what is given by the organization. Pay dissatisfaction occurs when the amount the person receives is perceived to be less than the amount the person feels he or she should receive (Gomez-Mejia, 1984). Lawler (1971) theorized that the smaller the difference between what is expected and the actual pay received, the higher the level of satisfaction.

Given that organizations have limited compensation resources, what is distributed at the top is not available for those near the bottom, so the lower one is in the distribution hierarchy, the lower the prestige, status, and economic benefits conferred by pay (Bloom, 1999). High-income people have high levels of pay satisfaction, so the higher the compensation level, the higher pay satisfaction (Pfeffer & Langston, 1993). Tang et al. (2004) report that what leads to pay satisfaction is not so much absolute salary but comparative salary. Tang, Tang and Homaifar (2006) write that high pay satisfaction is a result of those who have fair or high (internal and external) equity comparison. So, if my salary goes up dramatically, and that of my comparison group does, there is no change in my behavior (Furnham, 2005). The relationship of income to pay satisfaction depends on one's love of money and comparison (Tang, 2006). According to Tang and Chin (2003) those with low levels of the love of money have high levels of pay satisfaction. Employees with high levels of pay satisfaction are least likely to participate in evil or unethical behavior in the workplace (Tang and Chin, 2003). Tang, Kim and Tang (2002) write that pay satisfaction maybe high if the importance of money is not increased and if one's pay is not compared to others. Sweeney and McFarlin (2005) state that if the comparison of pay is positive or negative to similar others then the result is pay satisfaction or dissatisfaction. However, inside comparison maybe more important than outside comparison in predicting pay satisfaction (Sweeney & McFarlin, 2005).

According to Furnham (2005), no matter what people are paid, if they believe, with or without evidence that they are not equitably and fairly paid, they become de-motivated. Merriman (2005) reported that there are circumstances or situations that lower highly paid employees pay satisfaction.

Previous research demonstrates that pay dissatisfaction is related to reduce employee performance (Bretz & Thomas, 1992). According to Heneman and Judge (2000) pay dissatisfaction can have an impact on a variety of desirable employee outcomes (p. 85). Furnham (2006) writes that business psychologist site at least four reasons why money is likely to cause dissatisfaction than satisfaction. First, no clear correlation exists between pay and performance. Second, comparative salary leads to pay satisfaction not necessarily absolute salary. Third, lifestyle gains maybe more attractive than financial rewards. Finally, a salary increases with implication of increased taxes loses the luster of the pay rise (Furnham, 2006). Sweeney and McFarlin (2005) in their study of wage comparisons found that actual pay was a predictor of pay satisfaction. Balkin and Gomez-Mejia (2002) in their study of 194 professors of management concluded that given all things being equal with regard to pay increases, male faculty experiencing dissatisfaction with pay left their institution.

Female faculties in the same study were satisfied with pay increases even if they knew it was lower than that of male faculty. Oshagbemi and Hickson (2003) investigated the relationship of overall job and pay satisfaction of full-time university teachers at 23 institutions in the UK. The study found that overall UK academic teachers were dissatisfied with their job and women were more satisfied than men with pay.

Currall, Towler, Judge and Kohn's (2005) study provided linkages between pay satisfaction and performance outcomes and concluded with three managerial implications relating to pay satisfaction. Managers should be aware of the impact that the following items have on pay satisfaction and performance outcomes: First, pay satisfaction has an impact on individual job performance and the linkage of the overall organizational performance, which can affect the organization's competitive position. Second, employees bundle their attitudes towards pay into one single overarching affective reaction to pay. Third, high rates of employee turnover are associated with low pay (Currall et al., 2005). In disagreement, Furnham (2006) states that little evidence exist that satisfaction leads to productivity. Managers would be wiser to invest in better productivity than satisfaction. The result is a productive employee that is better rewarded, positively appraised and has more confidence (Furnham, 2006). Satisfaction with one's pay has a significant impact on employees' feelings of worth to the organization.

Organizational Worth

This next section of the literature reviews previous research on organizational worth and includes the following topics: higher pay levels and the covenantal relationship.

Gardner, Dyne and Pierce (2004) identified overall pay level (as opposed to the most recent pay increase) as a signal of overall employee worth to the organization. Fair compensation practices are likely to signal that the organization cares for its employees and wishes to treat them well (Rhoades & Eisenberger, 2002). According to Bloom (2004) compensation systems also play important social and symbolic roles in organizations, and through these roles pay systems affect a variety of important outcomes such as the nature of work relationships, employee commitment, and performance. In agreement with this relational exchange, O'Reilly and Pfeffer (2000) believe that compensation systems determine if people feel they are treated fairly and if the organization is worthy of their commitment and highest efforts.

Higher pay levels signal to employees that they matter to the organization. Gardner et al.'s (2004) study demonstrated that employees who receive higher amounts of pay feel more highly valued by the organization, and those who feel valued highly are rated as higher performers. White and Mackenzie-Davey (2003) define feeling valued as "A positive affective response arising from confirmation, within a congruent set of criteria, of an individual's possession of the qualities on which worth or desirability depends" (p. 228). These researchers go further by stating that personal recognition of contributions made to the organization appears to be more important to feeling valued than pay (White & Mackenzie-Davey, 2003).

According to Barnett and Schubert (2002) employees will feel both valued by and value their organization if a covenantal relationship exists with the employer. A covenantal relationship is a specific type of relational contract with the organization (Barnett & Schubert, 2002). This type of relationship requires both parties to do whatever is necessary to uphold commonly held values with a mutually agreed upon pledge (Barnett & Schubert, 2002). Employees who feel a sense of closeness or tie to the organization maybe better equip to perform on the job.

Job Performance

This second section of the literature reviews previous research on job performance and includes several related topics: Studies on definitions and measures of Job Performance and Performance Levels.

Researchers provided evidence that pay has a direct effect on performance (Gneezy & Rustichini, 2000; Hechler & Wiener, 1974). However, according to Vroom (1964) and Lawler (1971) money as a motivator of performance must be perceived by the worker as instrumental to receiving the money. In other words, pay is seen as dependent upon performance. According to Stiffler (2006a) pay-for-performance programs must motivate employees to perform in their jobs and reinforce behaviors associated with organizational and job related behaviors. The message sent by pay-for-performance programs from management is that employee contributions are appreciated and valued (Stiffler, 2006b).

Deci (1972) writes that it is not necessarily the money which motivates performance but how it is administered. If money is used as a motivator or controller of performance it must be administered contingently. Kauhanen and Piekkola (2006) studied performance-related pay schemes. The result of there study concluded that performance-related pay (PRP) has a positive effect on motivation of highly educated employees. The study further found that performance measures should be known, level of payment should be high enough and payments should be made frequently (Kauhanen & Piekkola, 2006).

Performance contingent pay has been investigated by many scholars. According to Bishop (1987) tying wages to productivity may benefit the firm in three ways: "First, it serves as an incentive for greater effort. Second, it tends to attract to the firm more able workers and those who like to work hard…Third, it reduces the probability of losing the best performers to other firms and raises the probability that the least productive workers will leave" (p.37). Researchers provide evidence that positive outcomes such as higher subsequent performance are more likely when pay increases are made contingent on good performance than when pay increases are not contingent on performance (Gerhart & Milkovich, 1992; Jenkins, Mitra, Gupta & Shaw, 1998). Rynes et al. (2004) agree with the concept by asserting that pay is contingent on performance as a direct motivator.

Merit pay has been linked to many pay for performance contingency programs. Merit pay plans are pre-determined standards that are well-communicated providing a greater reward for those performing at higher levels (Schulz & Tanguay, 2006). According to Barclay and York (2003) merit systems can only be effective if the relationship of the systems to business objectives, as well as merit pay dependence on variations of performance appraisal is considered by the organization. A study conducted by Barclay and York (2003) of three judges who made merit pay decisions for 36 faculties in a public university business school concluded that for their judgment on research, teaching, and service greater weight for merit increases was placed primarily on research. This is interesting to the researchers because if faculty placed all their efforts into research, the university would have a difficulty time providing excellent teaching or community service, two of the major business objectives (Barclay & York, 2003). Marchant and Newman's (1994) study of the heads of education divisions at 245 colleges and universities found that deans viewed merit pay, contract renewal, tenure and promotion at a high ranking as motivators than did the department heads. The goal of merit pay is to tie the organizations goals with that of the employee. Those employees who perform at their peak performance are rewarded for their efforts. Hellerman, Kochanski, Adwin and Wong (2007) write that merit pay plans can be worth the challenge and provide tested ideas. First, view merit pay as an investment earned though on the job performance. Second, focus on performance though messages that "performance counts." Third, aggregate merit budgets though clear standards that distinguish top performance from expected performance. Fourth, use cross-unit calibration across managers for fairness. Finally, create a set-aside pool for top performers (Hellerman, Kochanski, Adwin & Wong, 2007). Nelson (1997) states that some believe within academia all university salaries should be the same, that accomplishments (performance) are irrelevant.

Merit pay like any other pay for performance plan should provide employees with feedback necessary to improve performance, thus increasing merit rewards.

According to Mawhinney and Gowen (1990) operant conditioning theory states that the importance of the amount and timing of the reward are important to employees' response of merit pay. Organizations that desire superior employee performance that is rewarded through incentives can use merit pay like systems to meet their objective. However, organizations must remember that employees do not perform at the same level and thus a measurement should be in place to accurately measure contributions (Mawhinney & Gowen, 1990).

The research on job performance has focused on merit pay as a way to recognize performance in faculty in both private and public institutions. Schulz and Tanguay (2006) state that the ongoing argument against merit pay plans in public educational institutions is that academic work makes the design and implementation of a successful plan difficult. This is due in part to the three traditional evaluations of merit pay plans; teaching, research and service that is complex to assess (Kasten, 1984). Add to these concerns the opinion by some that public university merit pay plans discriminate against specific faculty members (Schulz & Tanguay, 2006). According to Magnusen (1987) administrators within academic institutions can assist public university success of merit pay by developing pay systems that align faculty contributions with university's strategic goals. In Schulz and Tanguay (2006) study of 486 full-time unionized faculty of the university sampled to assess the relationship of teaching, research and service to report merit pay it was found that self-reported scholarship activities was predictive of receipt of merit pay not service or teaching. A second important finding of this study, found that females had significantly less support than male colleagues for merit pay systems as a means of rewarding performance, thus suggesting a strong distrust (Schulz & Tanguay, 2006).

Researchers Terpstra and Honoree (2005) share opposing opinions of the effects of merit pay incentive plan as poorly designed leading to perceptions of unfairness and inequity for individuals. The result is perceptions of inequity that have a negative impact on important organizational outcomes (Terpstra & Honoree, 2005). Terpstra and Honoree's (2005) study of 490 faculties revealed that the typical response to merit pay inequity was to leave their jobs in an attempt to restore equity. As a result, turnover and replacement cost would be high for some organizations, not to mention the best performers quit, leaving only the mediocre and poor individuals. The study did not find a difference in the way men and women responded to perceived merit pay inequities, however, the suggestion was made by the researchers that employees must believe their pay is based solely on merit (Terpstra & Honoree, 2005). In agreement, Lawler and Worley (2006) state that merit-pay plans do not motivate performance or help retain the right employee. In fact, due to the typically small salary increases of merit-pay plans the relationship of pay and performance is weak and not motivational (Lawler & Worley, 2006). A study by the U.S. Merit Systems Protection Board found pay-for-performance plans do not always achieve desired outcomes due to error in design, implementation or usage (Petrimoulx, 2007). The board further states that the change from tenure-based to pay-for-performance base is not easy, no one best way exist for designing pay-for-performance systems and pay-for-performance systems may not be appropriate for all organizations (Petrimoulx, 2007).

According to Thompson (1980) people are the key to the performance of any business; PCSE (participation, communication, sharing, information and enrichment) is the way to turn the key for profitability. In most instances, employee performance is determined by three things: (1) ability; (2) the work environment; and (3) motivation (Griffin, 1990, p. 437). Nelson (2006) writes that workers can't perform if they don't know what to do or how to do it. Managers are there to support worker performance by valuing finished work, as well as efforts by workers to do the job well (Nelson, 2006). According to Nelson (2006) workers that feel unappreciated are likely to quit. The manager's challenge is to have the goals of the employee and those of the company coincide (McFillen & Podsakoff, 1983). To do this effectively, the manager must view the issues from the perspective of the one being motivated, not the one trying to do the motivation (McFillen & Podsakoff, p. 48). Managers should realize that all employees are motivated but not all employees are motivated to do what the manager wants. Will the performance desired by the manager result in rewards desired by the employee? "Does performance result in outcomes that non-performance does not" (McFillen & Podsakoff, p.49)? Perry, Mesch and Paarlberg (2006) concluded in there study that there is much to learn about human performance and financial incentives for employees.

The success of performance management systems must tap into the key determinates of employee motivation (Bradt, 1996). According to Trahant (2007) strong performance management systems support organizational alignment, clear line of sight and employee empowerment. Stiffler (2006) writes that motivation to achieve individual goals should be tied to individual performance. In agreement with organizational behaviorists, Siggins (1993) states that a connection exists between work-related attitude and employee job performance. Samad's (2005) study concluded that both organizational commitment and job satisfaction relate to increased job performance. According to Bradt (1996) as far back as the 1920s, researchers established that the ability to see progress toward a goal and to know the results of actions had major impact on employee performance.

Past job performance is the best predictor for future job performance is practically a human resource dogma. According to Stuman, Cheramie and Cashen (2002).employee job performance changes, experience is acquired, motivation is gained or lost and opportunities are presented to succeed or fail. Reinforcement theorists argue that increases in performance following monetary rewards suggest that pay is a positive reinforcer (Gerhart, Minkoff & Olsen, 1995). Research in which scholars have investigated the effects of incentive pay reflects the reinforcement ideas that "the more closely pay is tied to performance, the more powerful its motivational effect" (Guzzo & Katzell, 1987). According to Sammer (2007) employees must see a clear linkage between their efforts and incentive payouts to change their behavior or improve performance. Teach (2006) writes that many believe the link between productivity and pay is broken. Employees are working harder but not necessarily reaping the rewards of their efforts (Teach, 2006). Lawler and Worley (2006) state that organizations that want to motivate performance and change with cash should use bonuses.

By providing a better understanding of what drives employees to perform, employers are able to energize or motivate the employee to meet the organizational overall performance outcome.

Performance Levels

This section reviews previous research on performance levels and include several related topics: Studies on pay dispersion and high achievers.

Stuman, Trevor, Boudreau and Gerhart's (2003) research focuses on a different type of pay decision – how to allocate pay increases across employees at different performance levels. Ultimately, as employees increase levels of performance they have a greater change of achieving larger pay dispersion, which would help the organization keep high achievers and weed out the underachievers. Additionally, the organization would have a competitive advantage as high performance levels would translate to increased output of productivity. "Pay dispersion may increase effort and provide incentives for high workforce performance levels, but may also inhibit cooperation and goal orientation among employees" (Shaw, Gupta & Delery, 2002, p. 461).

To the contrary, Deutsch (1985) argued that pay dispersion diminishes performance by reducing cooperation among employees. In agreement, Bloom (1999) also suggests that high pay dispersion may reduce organizational performance. He notes that organizational performance goes beyond the sum of individual performances of its members, but often requires collaboration and commitment of common goals (Gardner, 1999). According to Gardner (1999) Bloom suggested two possible explanations: First, pay dispersion among employees should be kept to a minimum to encourage teamwork. Second, perception of pay inequity can inhibit a high level of performance.

The results of Bloom's (1999) study indicate greater pay dispersion of the organization has a direct association with lower individual and group performance, at least where work interdependencies are important. Similarly, Frick, Prinz and Winkelmann (2003) examined wage dispersion as it relates to performance of sports teams. The results demonstrated that based on the situation wage inequality of teams can have an effect on performance (Frick et al., 2003). The motivating aspects of pay dispersion can only be understood when accompanied by legitimate or normatively acted factors (Shaw, et al., 2002). Shaw et al. (2002) summarized a variety of theoretical perspectives supporting the argument that pay dispersion is motivation enhancing and results in higher levels of workforce performance, but these benefits are associated with the use of individual incentives. Pay dispersion in the absence of individual incentives is likely to weaken performance-reward linkages and valences (individual motivation theories), diminish the perceived legitimacy of the system (institutional theory), and violate rules of consistency and control (organizational justice theory) (p. 493). They go further to state, that when employees do not have to rely on one another to accomplish work, individual incentives provide the motivational stimulus for increasing effort and higher levels in the pay distribution (Shaw et., 2002).

Trank, Rynes and Bretz (2002) argue that high social achievers are likely not only to expect more challenging work and more rapid promotions but also higher pay levels and larger performance bonuses. Previous research has shown that high achievers would have stronger preferences than others for pay systems-based on individual rather than group performance (Trank et al., 2002). Moreover, these researchers show that high achievers may differentiate themselves by placing a higher value on performance feedback than other applicants. To support this, McClelland Atkinson, Clark and Lowell (1953) state that high achievement individuals tend to have received extensive performance feedback as children and desire similar levels of performance feedback as adults.

Ideally, if all that is needed is a link between performance and monetary rewards as these researchers have stated, then organization may need to award compensation solely on the basis of what is done by the employee over a length of time and not years of service. Yet there are those who argue that pay for performance is a de-motivator rather than a motivator.

Employees who are considered high performers in the organizations are perceived by most employers to be satisfied with their jobs. Effective performance leads to job satisfaction (Lawler & Porter, 1967).

Job Satisfaction

This final section of the literature reviews previous research on job satisfaction and includes several related topics: Studies on definitions and measures of Job Satisfaction and Environmental Influences.

Job satisfaction, like performance and attitude towards money and work, is a multifaceted and emotional attitude. Morse (1953) and Porter (1962) view satisfaction as the result that job needs are being fulfilled. According to Brief (1998) one can think about a satisfying job as both the degree to which it facilitates the attainment of those terminal values most important to a person and the degree to which it allows or encourages behaviors consistent with those instrumental values most important to the person (p. 18). The sum of job satisfaction is the evaluation of the discriminable elements of which the job is composed (Locke, 1969). Milbourn and Haight (2004) reveal that a person with job satisfaction (high level) holds a positive attitude about the job, as apposed to a person who is dissatisfied with his or her job. According to Bedeian, et al., (1992) when the same phenomenon (job satisfaction) is viewed through different "lenses" one does "see" different things. Job satisfaction is, therefore; seen by some people to be a function of what is expected and what is received. Thus, if one expects little and gets little, one will be satisfied. At the same time, if one expects a great deal and gets a great deal, one will also be satisfied. However, if one expects a great deal but gets little, one will be dissatisfied (Oshagbemi, 2000).

When dissatisfied, some employees may quit, others may complain, steal, disrupt teamwork, or be insubordinate (Cranny, Smith and Stone, 1992). According to Tang (2006) a contributor to low job satisfaction is low pay satisfaction because job satisfaction consists of satisfaction with work, pay, promotions, supervision and coworkers. For some people the love of money leads to job dissatisfaction (Tang, 2006). Dissatisfaction factors can sometimes be beyond the manager or staff control such as budget restrictions, poor administrative leadership or inadequate equipment (Siggins, 1993). Schaffer (1953) believed individual overall job satisfaction is dependent on who can be satisfied and are satisfied. Within a university work environment, it was found that of eight aspects of job satisfaction, workers were most dissatisfied with their pay and promotions (Oshagbemi, 1995, 1996). According to Oshagbemi (2000) we therefore, need to know a great deal more about the determination and importance of pay to workers before management can be sure of influencing decisions about pay through personnel policies and procedures. One view of job satisfaction holds that women are satisfied with jobs in which they can interact with others in a supportive and cooperative way, even though the jobs may be only minimally demanding and challenging (Mason, 1995). The organizational policies and practices need to focus on providing managerial women with opportunities for responsibility, advancement, achievement and challenging work if companies want to reap the benefits of the managerial women's skills and expertise (Mason, 1995). Bilimoria, Perry, Liang, Stroller, Higgins and Taylor (2006) conducted a study to determine academic job satisfaction of male and female faculty at a research university. The result of the study concluded that both male and female believe that leadership and mentoring influence their job satisfaction; however, for women internal relational support perceptions were much more important than academic job satisfaction. Barnett and Rivers (2004) write that research does not support the idea that women are more relational than men according to a study conducted by Purdue University.

Saari and Judge (2004) state that organizations only have so much control of employee satisfaction as it is a result of spillover into life satisfaction. Llorente and Macias (2005) write that job satisfaction goes hand in hand with the fit between the objective conditions of the job and the worker's expectation. Expectation and job reality determine greater job satisfaction.

In order to retain valued top performers, organizations must recognize that job satisfaction is indeed important and must be maintained. However, job satisfaction without appropriate compensation will lead the best and brightest into the arms of the competitors. Tang (2006) writes in his research that in order for the job satisfaction to income relationship to exist, one's income must be strongly related to work.

Falcone (2006) states that it is not necessarily employee job satisfaction that's at issue as much as employee engagement. Recognition and appreciation for a job well done will keep employees engaged. According to Charles H. Watts a consulting firm in Boston, employee engagement can make a difference in employee performance (Bates, 2004). Engagement relates to how the employee feels about his or her work experience and how they are treated (Bates, 2004). Organization must help employees to better themselves while benefiting the company and employees will be both satisfied and engaged (Falcone, 2006).

When some people think about satisfaction, they do not think about it in terms of feeling good; instead, they view satisfaction as the absence of feeling bad (Crow & Hartman, 1995). An example is Hackman and Oldham's (1980) discussion of a worker's reaction when asked if he liked his work. In effect, he responded that he gave the company a good day's work (in his view, at least!) in return for a fair day's pay. The worker did not respond that job satisfaction was the main factor but referred to pay. Job satisfaction of some employees over a length of time in the organization could be due in part to previous socialization or employment influences from past experiences.

Environmental Influences

Research supports the idea that job satisfaction is due in part to environmental influences. Staw and Ross (1985) suggest that job attitudes may reflect biologically-based trait which influences the information individuals input, recall and interpret within social or work situations. According to Saari and Judge (2004) a good match between employees and jobs will ensure people are placed into appropriate jobs, thus enhancing job satisfaction.

In a later study, Staw, Bell and Clausen (1986) found evidence that affective dispositions influence job attitudes over long periods of time. Gerhardt (1987) also found that disposition factors are associated with job satisfaction. Avery et al. (1989) reported that genetic and socialization factors contributed to approximately 30% of general feelings of job satisfaction. If job satisfaction or dissatisfaction is a predisposition as these researchers report then it is unlikely that organizations can change the "happiness" of its employees with money. However, there is empirical evidence that coworker relations are also an antecedent of job satisfaction (Morrison, 2004). Environmental influences, such as, socialization and previous employment experiences may indeed pay a major role in how employees view money; performance on the job and the resulting satisfaction within the organization.

Summary

The literature review illustrates that researchers have different but compelling views on monetary motivation as a vehicle to increase job performance and job satisfaction.

However, there is no considerable controversy regarding how money is viewed and used in attracting, rewarding, recognizing, motivating, retaining and punishing employees within organizations. What has been criticized is the employers' lack of insight into what employees want and need in the employment relationship. Some researchers believe that a climate must be created for the employee to perform, whilst others believe that the organization must know the personal objectives of employees before the organization can accomplish productivity objectives.

Furthermore, researchers have stated that employees compare themselves to others on the job to determine their level of outcome. If the employee perceives inequity steps are taken to change input and can result in tension, turnover, theft and lower productivity. Women on average earn less than men despite their advantages in education and work experience. The wage gap can be viewed as unfair and a contributor to issues of discrimination in higher education.

The review by researchers is mixed on the benefits of extrinsic incentives to promote performance and satisfaction. On one hand, financial distress of employees can lead to lost productivity. On the other hand, employers who provide access to financial programs will benefit and reduce financial stress for employees leading to increased productivity.

Employees ultimately expect compensation that is fair and comparable when determining satisfaction or dissatisfaction. Dissatisfaction with pay leads to demotivation, reduced performance and sends a clear message of organizational worth to the employees.

Demographic variables regarding age, gender, tenure, and educational level may influence both job performance and job satisfaction. Thus, this study examines the relationship of monetary motivation (money attitudes) and both job performance and job satisfaction. The next chapter of this study will focus on the research design and methodology of this study.

CHAPTER THREE

III - METHODOLOGY

This chapter will define the research design and methodology for this study. More specifically, it describes the corresponding population and sample, the research variables and relationship of variables, operational definitions, survey instruments, reliability and validity, data collection procedure, research questions with their respective hypotheses, data analysis and strategy and the limitations of the study.

Research Design of the Study

The research design of the study is a quantitative survey research to assess whether monetary motivation at multicultural for-profit institutions of higher learning will lead to an increase in job performance and job satisfaction. The purpose of the study is to explore the relationship between monetary motivation as measured by money attitudes and its effect on increased job performance and job satisfaction.

> As long as pay is valued and as long as employees accurately perceive the connection between pay and performance, actually tying pay more closely to performance should lead to stronger motivation to perform effectively (Lawler, 1971.p. 118).

> Economists and many executives are prone to stress the importance of the size of the pay check in determining a worker's job satisfaction and the probability that he will remain on his job (Vroom, 1982, p. 150).

The research model of the study appears in Figure 2, which depicts the proposed relationships among the variables or constructs "Monetary Motivation, Job Performance and Job Satisfaction."

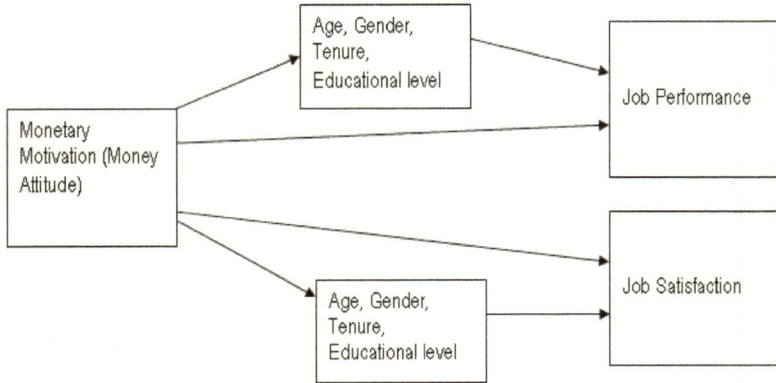

Figure 2 - The Relationship between Monetary Motivation (Money Attitudes), increased Job Performance and Job Satisfaction

Corresponding Population and Sample

The target population for the study is students and employees at multicultural for-profit institutions of higher learning across the United States. For-profit institutions regionally have been plagued over the last few years in the media with complaints from former students and employees regarding their finances and business practices. This continued focus on the for-profit industry in higher education has led accrediting bodies, such as the Southern Association of Colleges and Schools (SACS) to examine and question why the student body and employees are leaving in record numbers. The for-profit institutions were chosen because they are large enough to support this research and they are faced daily with voluntary and involuntary turnover of students and employees. From the population, a convenience sample of students and employees from specific for-profit institutions are used for this research. Participants will be online students completing a degree program and full-time and part-time employees working within the university system. The sample will include workers from a wide varied of work experience and positions within their various organizations. The respondents are ensured of anonymity of their responses.

Research Variables

Variables are measurements of characteristics, qualities, or ideas used in hypothesis testing (Sims, 2000, pp. 94).

The independent variable for this study is monetary motivation measured by money attitudes, as measured by the Money Ethic Scale short form (good, evil, achievement, respect, budget and freedom/power).

The dependent variables for this study are job performance and job satisfaction. The factor representing job performance is the Job Involvement Scale ("an individual's values towards work in general, the extent to which the person wants to perform well in a particular job and the extent to which individuals personally identify with their work"). The factor representing job satisfaction is the Minnesota Satisfaction Questionnaire (extrinsic and intrinsic rewards, working conditions and co-workers).

Relationship of Variables and Definitions

The literature review proposes that a relationship exists between monetary motivation, job performance and job satisfaction and that relationship is depicted in Figure 1 and 2.

Certain terms which are to be utilized in this work will need further clarification as to their meaning and measure.

Money. According to Furnham and Argyle (1998) money is a medium of exchange and has objective functions. It can be used to acquire goods and services and as a unit of account. Money is also a store of value and a standard of deferred payment. The most obvious way that money is used in the employee-organization relationship is that companies pay employees in exchange for their labor (Mitchell & Mickel, 1999).

Motivation. Vroom (1964) defined motivation as processes governed by personal choices as an alternate to other activities. Vroom's Expectancy Theory postulates that motivation is determined by three factors: (1) the perception that effort will result in success; (2) the perception that a successful performance will lead to a valued outcome - a reward of some kind; (3) and that personal satisfaction will be derived from the outcome. All three elements must be present for an individual to be motivated (Capstone Encyclopaedia of Business, 2003).

Work or Employment Work. According to Jaques (1961) employment work is the functions to be performed that are specified by an employer who pays the role occupant (employee) a wage or salary for his or her services.

Extrinsic Rewards. Mathis and Jackson (2000) define extrinsic rewards as tangible and have the form of both monetary and nonmonetary rewards (pp.416). The dictionary of Human Resources and Personnel Management (1997) defines extrinsic rewards as financial or material reward for work that can be measured, whereas intrinsic rewards cannot.

Pay Satisfaction. Pay satisfaction is a result of what the employee expects to receive as opposed to what is given by the organization (Lawler, 1971, 1981).

Employee. An employee for the purpose of this study is defined as a person who works under a contract of employment (Rubery, Earnshaw, Marchington, Cooke & Vincent, 2002).

Job Performance. Job performance is defined for the purpose of this study as the action, behaviors and outcomes engaged in by employees that are linked and contribute to organizational goals (Viswesvaran & Ones, 2000).

Job Satisfaction. Flanagan, Strauss and Ulman (1974) define job satisfaction as the pleasure an individual derives from his or her work. Factors that affect job satisfaction include pay, working hours, complexity and difficulty of job, promotion prospects and personal relationships with co-workers.

Multicultural. Multicultural is defined for the purpose of this study as a diverse population that includes several cultures and or ethnic groups (Canen & Canen, 2001).

For-Profit Institution. For the purpose of this research for-profit institutions are established and operate for the sole purpose of making a profit (Kinser & Levy, 2005).

Survey Instruments

The continuous measures used in this study were obtained from the Money Ethic Scale (Tang, 1992) and research questionnaires in Cook, Hepworth, Wall, and Warr (1981) reference book entitled *The Experience of Work*. The final questionnaire consists of 41 items relating to monetary motivation, job performance and job satisfaction and 6 demographical items relating to current status, age, gender, tenure and educational level. A Likert- scale is used for the scales measuring the constructs. The measures used to operationalize (assess) the constructs in the research models are described below.

Monetary Motivation. The independent variable in the research model monetary motivation is measured with money attitudes. The survey instrument used for monetary motivation is the short form of the Money Ethic Scale (MES). The purpose of the MES is to measure money attitudes in organization and work settings. The original Money Ethic Scale (MES) contained 50 items and used a seven-point response dimension. Tang (1992) developed the scale based on previous research written about money. Several different versions of the short form MES have been used by others in their research (Dunford, Boudreau & Boswell; 2005, Mitchell & Mickel; 1999, Tang, Kim & Tang; 2002, Thozhur, Riley & Szivas; 2006 and Vitell, Paolillo & Singh; 2006). This study will use the short form of the MES that contains 12 questions. For the purpose of this study the MES short form will use a five-point Likert scale response dimension. Those responses will be strongly agree, agree, neutral, disagree and strongly disagree; scored 1 to 5 respectively and summation calculated.

The factors on the MES short form that address "good or positive attitudes" are 4 and 8; questions addressing "evil" are 11 and 12; questions addressing "achievement" are 1 and 3, questions addressing "respect or self-esteem" are 2 and 5, questions addressing "budget" are 9 and 10 and questions addressing "freedom or power" are 6 and 7.

Dunford, Boudreau and Boswell (2005) studied underwater stock option value and executive job search and retention using the short form 8 item Money Ethic

Scale (MES). The study found no relationship between money success perceptions, percentage of options underwater and job search for executives.

Table 2 - Monetary Motivation Measurement Questions

Short Form - Money Ethic Scale (MES)
1. Money is a symbol of success (A)
2. Money will help you express your competence and abilities (R)
3. Money represents one's achievement (A)
4. I value money very highly (G)
5. Money makes people respect you in the community (R)
6. Money can give you the opportunity to be what you want to be (F)
7. Money gives you autonomy and freedom (F)
8. Money is important (G)
9. I budget my money very well (B)
10. I use my money very carefully (B)
11. Money is the root of all evil (E)
12. Money is evil (E)

Tang, Kim and Tang (2002) used the short form 6 item Money Ethic Scale (MES) to study full-time employees, part-time employed students and non-employed university students in the southeastern United States. They found that attitudes towards money were not related to pay satisfaction. Non-employed students did not feel strongly about money as a measure of success, money was budgeted carefully and that money is not evil compared to part-time employees.

Thozhur, Riley and Szivas (2006) distributed the short form 12 item Money Ethic Scale (MES) to blue-collar employees identified as low paid based on industry and occupation according to The National Minimum Wage Commission in the United Kingdom. The study found that pay satisfaction of low paid employees was determined by individual differences in money attitudes.

Job Performance. The dependent variable in the research model job performance is measured with work-related attitudes towards job performance. The survey instrument used for job performance is the short form Job Involvement Scale (Cammann, Fichman, Jenkins & Klesh, 1979; Lodahl & Kejner, 1965). The purpose of the JIS (Lodahl & Kejner, 1965) is to measure an individual's value towards work (work involvement) and the extent that individual wants to perform well (job motivation). The original Job Involvement Scale (JIS) contain 110 items reduced to 20 items then 6 and finally 4 items (Lodahl and Kejner, 1965). Cammann, Fichman, Jenkins and Klesh (1979) study assess the extent to which individuals personally identify with their work and contained 3 items adapted from Lodahl and Kejner's (1965) measure. Several researchers have used a wide-ranging choice of scale items and response dimensions of the original Job Involvement scale (Cummings & Bigelow; 1976, Jones, James & Bruni; 1975, and Morris & Snyder; 1979).

This study will use the short form of the JIS that contains 9 questions and a five-point Likert scale response dimension. Those responses will be strongly agree, agree, neutral, disagree and strongly disagree; scored 1 to 5 respectively and summation calculated.

Table 3 - Job Performance Measurement Questions

Short Form – Job Involvement Scale (JIS)

1. I'll stay overtime to finish a job, even if I'm not paid for it
2. The major satisfaction in my life comes from my job
3. For me, mornings at work really fly by
4. I usually show up for work a little early, to get things ready
5. The most important things that happen to me involve my work
6. I'm really a perfectionist about my work
7. I feel depressed when I fail at something connected with my job
8. I live, eat and breathe my job
9. I would probably keep working even if I didn't need the money

----

Chan (2007) studied leader communication skills and motivating language approaches as it relates to subordinates job satisfaction using the JIS in a unionized job setting. The study found a linkage exists between all variables.

Capon and Chernyshenko (2007) studied army individuals in the New Zealand Army using the JIS. The study found that work satisfaction and organizational commitment mediate the relationship of intention to remain and job involvement.

Kelloway, Catano and Carroll (2000) distributed an adapted JIS to 233 union stewards in a provincial government employees union to identify the relationship between psychological involvement in the union, conflict between the union and family responsibilities. The study found a significant relationship existed.

Kuhnert and Palmer (1991) used the short form JIS to study 104 employees of a large state agency. The study found a relationship between intrinsic and extrinsic work factors. A significant relationship did exist for intrinsic factors.

Job Satisfaction. The dependent variable in the research model to measure work related attitudes toward overall job satisfaction employed in the present research is the Minnesota Satisfaction Questionnaire short form (MSQ). The purpose of the MSQ is to measure intrinsic, extrinsic and overall job satisfaction identified by "I" and "E" in the scale (Weiss, Dawis, England and Lofquist, 1967).

The instrument is composed of 20 items all of which was used in this study to cover extrinsic (questions 5-6, 12-14 and 19), intrinsic (questions 1-4, 7-11, 15-16 and 20), working conditions (question 17) and co-workers (question 18) job satisfaction. Respondents will use a five point measurement to access their satisfaction or dissatisfaction with their job. Those responses are: very dissatisfied;

dissatisfied; I can't decide whether I am satisfied or not; satisfied; very satisfied; respectively scored 1-5 and summation calculated (Cook et al., 1981).

Table 4 - Overall Job Satisfaction Measurement Questions

Short Form - Minnesota Satisfaction Questionnaire (MSQ)

On my present job, this is how I feel about:
1. Being able to keep busy all the time (I)
2. The chance to work alone on the job (I)
3. The chance to do different things from time to time (I)
4. The chance to be "somebody" in the community (I)
5. The way my boss handles employees (E)
6. The competence of my supervisor in making decisions (E)
7. Being able to do things that don't go against my conscience (I)
8. The way my job provides for steady employment (I)
9. The chance to do things for other people (I)
10. The chance to tell people what to do (I)
11. The chance to do something that makes use of my abilities (I)
12. The way company policies are put into practice (E)
13. My pay and the amount of work I do (E)
14. The chances for advancement on this job (E)
15. The freedom to use my own judgment (I)
16. The chance to try my own methods of doing the job (I)
17. The working conditions (Working conditions)
18. The way my co-workers get along with each other (Co-workers)
19. The praise I get for doing a good job (E)
20. The feeling of accomplishment I get form the job (I)

Alexander (2004) used the short form of the MSQ to study 147 African American male ministers within the continental USA. The study found no significant relationship of job satisfaction for age, tenure, affective commitment and continuance. A significant relationship did exist between job satisfaction and normative commitment.

Kinnoin (2005) studied both undergraduate and graduate students who attended school and worked from a university in southern California using the MSQ short form. The study found greater job satisfaction for companies that offered family-friendly policies.

Udechukwu (2007) distributed the short form MSQ to correctional officers in the southeast to determine intrinsic and extrinsic satisfaction related to leave behavior. The study found for both male and female officers intrinsic and extrinsic satisfaction was important.

Reliability and Validity

Reliability refers to whether a particular technique measured repeatedly of the same object, consistently yields the same results (Babbie, 2004). Sims (2000) states that a coefficient alpha of at least 0.70 is considered reliable for use in hypothesis testing (p. 60). Anderson, Anderson, Tatham and Black (1998) refer to validity as: "Extent to which a measure or set of measures correctly represents the concept of the study – the degree to which it is free from any systematic or non-random error" (p. 3). The reliability and validity of the survey instruments used in this study are explained.

The Money Ethic Scale short form (MES) measures money attitudes in organization and work settings. The factors on the MES address: 1). Good or positive attitudes, 2). Evil, 3). Achievement, 4). Respect or self-esteem, 5). Budget, 6). Freedom of power. The reliability and validity of the MES short form has been proven by various researchers.

Dunford, Boudreau and Boswell (2005) reported the MES 8 item scale reliability coefficient alpha of 0.85. Evidence of the MES convergent validity was shown as money success was positively related to job and pay satisfaction (Tang, 1995).

Thozhur, Riley and Szivas (2006) reported the MES 12 item scale reliability coefficient alpha of 0.72.

Vitell, Paolillo and Singh (2006) separated the scale into four separate dimensions and reported the MES 17 item scale reliability coefficient alpha as follows: important, 0.853; success, 0.823; motivator, 0.893 and rich, 0.880. The reliabilities for all are more than adequate as the alpha>0.70 (Nunnally, 1978).

The construct validity of the short form 12 item Money Ethic Scale (MES) was examined by comparing the MES 30 item scale with the six factors good, evil, achievement, respect, budget and freedom/power (Tang, 1995). Tang (1995) used the two factors with the highest item total correlation to develop the 12 items for the short MES scale. The research provided significant correlations between the long and short form MES scale factors: good (0.83), evil (0.84), achievement (0.85), respect (0.88), budget (0.91) and freedom/power (0.89) indicating the factors of the short MES scale is related to the long MES scale and appropriate as a measurement scale (Tang, 1995).

The Job Involvement Scale (JIS) short form measures an individual's value towards work (work involvement), the extent that individual wants to perform well (job motivation) and assess the extent to which individuals personally identify with their work (Cammann, Fichman, Jenkins and Klesh, 1979; Lodahl and Kejner, 1965). The reliability and validity of the short form JIS has been proven by various researchers: Chan (2007) reported the JIS 9 item scale reliability coefficient alpha of 0.63, Capon and Chernyshenko (2007) reported the JIS 6 item scale reliability coefficient alpha of 0.72, Kelloway, Catano and Carroll (2000) reported the JIS 6 item scale reliability coefficient alpha of 0.87 and Kuhnert and Palmer (1991) reported the JIS 3 item scale reliability coefficient alpha of 0.74. Ramsey, Lassk and Marshall (1995) reported a wide-ranging choice of the JIS 20 (0.79), 6 (0.70) and 4 (0.69) item scale reliability coefficient alpha.

The validity of the Job Involvement Scale (JIS) was shown to positively correlate with job satisfaction, job performance, intention to turn over and intrinsic and extrinsic motivation (Cammann et al., 1979; Lodahl and Kejner, 1965). The JIS is short, easily to completed and has face validity. Cook et al. (1981) provide research questionnaires including the JIS that have previously been tested and demonstrate validity.

The Minnesota Satisfaction Questionnaire (MSQ) short form measures measure intrinsic, extrinsic and overall job satisfaction. The reliability and validity of the short form MSQ has been proven by varies researchers: Kinnoin (2005) reported the MSQ 20 item scale reliability coefficient alpha of 0.92 and Udechukwu (2007) reported the MSQ 20 item scale internal consistency alpha of 0.88.

The validity of the short form MSQ is based on the results of the long form MSQ. To support or provide evidence for the short form MSQ the following are used: (1) The long form 100-item MSQ provided evidence of validity and the 20-item short form MSQ is a subscale of strong correlations of the long form MSQ; (2). Studies of intrinsic, extrinsic and general satisfaction; (3). Cook et al. (1981) provide research questionnaires including both the short and long form MSQ that have previously been tested and demonstrate validity.

Data Collection

This study will use three short form questionnaires: The Money Ethics Scale (MES) by Tang (1992), Job Involvement Scale (JIS) by Lodahl and Kejner (1965) and Cammann et al., (1979) and the Minnesota Satisfaction Questionnaire by Weiss, Dawis, England and Lofquist (1967).

The survey was entered into Zoomerang.com a web based tool and administered directly on the website. A survey invitation explaining the purpose of the study, content, directions for completion, how long the survey would take, assurance of confidentiality and the link to the website was provided.

Participants for the study are online students (full and part-time) and employees of universities and colleges. Access to a computer and some level of computer competency is required by participants to participate in the online survey. Reminders are automatically sent by Zoomerang to those participants that have not responded or partially completed the survey request.

Response or completion rates for studies using Zoomerang.com for online students (full or part-time) and employees of universities or colleges are not currently available.

Online surveys are relatively new but increasing in use due to the relative easy of use, price and convenience. Businesses are investigating the use of Zoomerang and other web based type surveys to make decisions about customers, products and price (Horowitz, 2004).

Horowitz (2004) writes that Zoomerang provides quantitative data that eliminates the use of phone surveys because it is accurate, cheaper to use and builds customer loyalty. In support of Zoomerang, Ward (2006) states that online surveys are less intrusive than a phone call which is why people are willing to participate. It is easier to create, distribute customize questions, compile and cross-tabulate the results due to the templates and software offered by Zoomerang, Question Pro, Qualtrics and others (Ward, 2006). Other recent supporters of online surveys include Evans and Mathur (2005) and Granello and Wheaton (2004).

Research Questions and Hypotheses

The following research questions will guide the hypotheses of this study:
- **Q1**. Is monetary motivation related to job performance at multicultural for-profit institutions of higher learning?
- **Q2**. Is monetary motivation related to job satisfaction at multicultural for-profit institutions of higher learning?

The following research hypotheses and null hypotheses will be examined in this study of the influence of monetary motivation on increased job performance and job satisfaction at multicultural for-profit institutions of higher learning:

Monetary Motivation will be measured with money attitudes. The survey instrument used for monetary motivation will be the short form Money Ethic Scale (MES) consisting of 12 questions (see Table 2 – Monetary Motivation Measurement questions developed by Tang (1992). The MES is an appropriate scale to measure money attitudes both in organizations and work settings (Dunford et al., 2005; Mitchell & Mickel, 1999; Tang et al., 2002; Thozhur et al., 2006 and Vitell et al., 2006).

H01: The effects of monetary motivation on job performance will decrease or have no effect with age at multicultural for-profit institutions of higher learning.

H1A: The effects of monetary motivation on job performance will increase or have no effect with age at multicultural for-profit institutions of higher learning.

Various researchers from the literature review (Bourne, 1982; Chu et al., 2001; McEvoy & Cascio, 1989) have provided support for this hypothesis, so it would follow that money attitudes on job performance would decrease or have no effect with age.

H02: The effects of monetary motivation on job satisfaction will decrease or have no affect with age at multicultural for-profit institutions of higher learning.

H2A: The effects of monetary motivation on job satisfaction will increase or have no effect with age at multicultural for-profit institutions of higher learning.

Various researchers from the literature review (Kauffman, 1987; Tu et al., 2005) have provided support for this hypothesis, so it would follow that money attitudes on job satisfaction would decrease or have no effect with age.

H03: The effects of monetary motivation on job performance will be higher for females than males at multicultural for-profit institutions of higher learning.

H3A: The effects of monetary motivation on job performance will be lower for females than males at multicultural for-profit institutions of higher learning.

Various researchers from the literature review (Tang et al., 2006; Taynor & Deaux, 1973, 1975) have provided support for this hypothesis, so it would follow that money attitudes on job performance would be higher for females than males.

H04: The effects of monetary motivation on job satisfaction will be higher for males than females at multicultural for-profit institutions of higher learning.

H4A: The effects of monetary motivation on job satisfaction will be lower for males than females at multicultural for-profit institutions of higher learning.

Various researchers from the literature review (Okpara et al., 2004; Tang & Talpade, 1999) have provided support for this hypothesis, so it would follow that money attitudes on job satisfaction would be higher for males than females.

H05: The effects of monetary motivation on job performance will increase with tenure at multicultural for-profit institutions of higher learning.

H5A: The effects of monetary motivation on job performance will decrease with tenure at multicultural for-profit institutions of higher learning.

Various researchers from the literature review (August et al., 2006; Barron, 2003) have provided support for this hypothesis, so it would follow that money attitudes on job performance will increase with tenure.

H06: The effects of monetary motivation on job satisfaction will increase with tenure at multicultural for-profit institutions of higher learning.

H6A: The effects of monetary motivation on job satisfaction will decrease with tenure at multicultural for-profit institutions of higher learning.

Various researchers from the literature review (Bedeian et al., 1992; Monk, 2007) have provided support for this hypothesis, so it would follow that money attitudes on job satisfaction will increase with tenure.

H07: The effects of monetary motivation on job performance will increase with educational level of the employee at multicultural for-profit institutions of higher learning.

H7A: The effects of monetary motivation on job performance will decrease with educational level of the employee at multicultural for-profit institutions of higher learning.

Various researchers from the literature review (Truxillo et al., 1998; Wise, 1975) have provided support for this hypothesis, so it would follow that money attitudes on job performance will increase with educational level.

H08: The effects of monetary motivation on job satisfaction will increase with educational level at multicultural for-profit institutions of higher learning.

H8A: The effects of monetary motivation on job satisfaction will decrease with educational level at multicultural for-profit institutions of higher learning.

Various researchers from the literature review (Allen & Velden, 2001; Gray & Chapman, 1999) have provided support for this hypothesis, so it would follow that money attitudes on job satisfaction will increase with educational level.

H09: The effects of monetary motivation on job performance will increase at multicultural for-profit institutions of higher learning.

H9A: The effects of monetary motivation on job performance will decrease at multicultural for-profit institutions of higher learning.

The measurement of work-related attitudes toward job performance is the short form Job Involvement Scale (JIS). The scale consist of 9 questions (see Table 3 – Job Performance Measurement Questions) developed by Lodahl and Kejner (1965) and Cammann et al., (1979). The JIS is an appropriate scale to measure an individual's value towards work (work involvement), the extent that individual wants to perform well (job motivation) and assess the extent to which individuals personally identify with their work (Chan, 2007; Capon & Chernyshenko, 2007; Kelloway et al., 2000; Kuhnert & Palmer; 1991).

H10: The effects of monetary motivation on job satisfaction will increase at multicultural for-profit institutions of higher learning.

H10A: The effects of monetary motivation on job satisfaction will decrease at multicultural for-profit institutions of higher learning.

The measurement of work-related attitudes toward overall job satisfaction will be the Minnesota Satisfaction Questionnaire short form (MSQ). The instrument is composed of 20 questions (see Table 4 – Overall Job Satisfaction Measurement Questions) developed by Weiss et al. (1965). The MSQ is an appropriate scale to measure intrinsic, extrinsic and overall job satisfaction (Alexander, 2004; Cook et al., 1981; Kinnoin, 2005; Udechukwu, 2007).

Table 5 - The Variables of Hypothesis Model Summary

Hypothesis	Variables	Operational Variables
H1	Monetary Motivation Job Performance	Money Ethic Scale (Tang, 1992)
	Age	Job Involvement Scale (Cammann et al.,1979; Lodahl and Kejner, 1965)
		Demographic
H2	Monetary Motivation Job Satisfaction	Money Ethic Scale (Tang, 1992)
	Age	Minnesota Satisfaction Questionnaire (Weiss et al, 1967)
		Demographic
H3	Monetary Motivation Job Performance	Money Ethic Scale (Tang, 1992)
	Gender	Job Involvement Scale (Cammann et al., 1979; Lodahl and Kejner, 1965)
		Demographic
H4	Monetary Motivation Job Satisfaction	Money Ethic Scale (Tang, 1992)
	Gender	Minnesota Satisfaction Questionnaire (Weiss et al, 1967)
		Demographic

H5	Monetary Motivation Job Performance	Money Ethic Scale (Tang, 1992)
	Tenure	Job Involvement Scale (Cammann et al., 1979; Lodahl and Kejner, 1965)
		Demographic
H6	Monetary Motivation Job Satisfaction	Money Ethic Scale (Tang, 1992)
	Tenure	Minnesota Satisfaction Questionnaire (Weiss et al, 1967)
		Demographic
H7	Monetary Motivation Job Performance	Money Ethic Scale (Tang, 1992)
	Educational Level	Job Involvement Scale (Cammann et al., 1979; Lodahl and Kejner, 1965)
		Demographic
H8	Monetary Motivation Job Satisfaction	Money Ethic Scale (Tang, 1992)
	Educational Level	Minnesota Satisfaction Questionnaire (Weiss et al, 1967)
		Demographic
H9	Monetary Motivation Job Performance	Money Ethic Scale (Tang, 1992)
		Job Involvement Scale (Cammann et al., 1979; Lodahl and Kejner, 1965)
H10	Monetary Motivation Job Satisfaction	Money Ethic Scale (Tang, 1992)
		Minnesota Satisfaction Questionnaire (Weiss et al, 1967)

Data Analysis and Strategy

The data gathered for this study using MES, JIS and MSQ will be analyzed using the Statistical Product and Service Solutions (SPSS) formally known as Statistical Package for Social Sciences version 12.0.

The three scales MES, JIS and MSQ will be used to measure the variables monetary motivation, job performance and job satisfaction as shown in Table 6. To describe the sample population, independent and dependent variable descriptive statistics will be used. To reveal the relationship between variables correlation analysis will be performed. Internal reliability of the survey instruments will be calculated using Cronbach coefficient alpha. Variables will be tested for normality and transformed if variables are not normal. The nominal variable "gender" will be classified as male or female. Interval variables will be classified as "age" 18-20, 21-30,31-40,41-50,51-60 and 61 and above; "tenure" 5 or less years, 6-15 years, 16-25 years and more than 25 years; "educational level" High School Diploma/GED, Some College, 4-year Degree, and Masters Degree or Above.

Table 6 - Test Hypothesis Model

Hypothesis	Variables	Test
H1	Monetary Motivation Job Performance Age	Money attitudes is influenced by age (young adults) with an orientation to see money as evil (Tang, 1992)
		Job performance is influenced by the age of the newly hired (Saks and Waldman, 1998).
H2	Monetary Motivation Job Satisfaction Age	Money attitudes of older adults is viewed as more budget friendly and less negative (Tang, 1992)
		Job satisfaction is influenced by the age of the higher education faculty (Tu, Plaisent, Bernard and Maguiraga, 2005)
H3	Monetary Motivation Job Performance Gender	Money attitudes is influenced by sex (gender) and frame of reference (Tang, 1992)
		Job performance is influenced by gender and moderates positive affect (Castro, Douglas, Hochwarter, Ferris and Frink, 2003).
H4	Monetary Motivation Job Satisfaction Gender	Money attitudes of male students is influenced by achievement and respect (Tang, 1993)
		Job satisfaction is influenced by the gender of university teachers (Okpara, Squillace and Erondu, 2005)

H5	Monetary Motivation Job Performance Tenure	Money attitudes of tenured professors has an influence on job performance (Leslie, 1998)
H6	Monetary Motivation Job Satisfaction Tenure	Money attitudes of long tenured professors has an influence on job satisfaction (Luna-Arocas and Tang, 2004)
H7	Monetary Motivation Job Performance Educational Level	Money attitudes of educated people are more controlled and less obsessed (Tang, 1995) Job performance is influenced by educational level (Truxillo, Bennett & Collins, 1998)
H8	Monetary Motivation Job Satisfaction Educational Level	Money attitudes of full/part-time employees and non-employed university students is influenced by educational level (Tang, Kim and Tang, 2002) Job satisfaction is influenced by educational level (Allen and Velden, 2001)
H9	Monetary Motivation Job Performance	Money attitudes is an important motivator for job performance in cultural settings (Gbadamosi and Joubert, 2005)
H10	Monetary Motivation Job Satisfaction	Money attitudes is influenced by job satisfaction of individuals in different money profiles (Tang, Tang and Luna-Aroca, 2005)

Assumptions and Limitations

The assumption is made that the data collection method will be appropriate for the sample population being studied and the respondents will be honest in their responses. This study is limited to students (full and part-time) and employees of for-profit higher learning institutions that are accustom to online surveys. Assumptions are made by the researcher that the responses will be of use in making generalities regarding the relationship between monetary motivation, job performance and job satisfaction. Conclusions drawn from the results of this study will be reflective of the limitations presented.

Summary

Chapter III presented the research design and methodology of the study including the corresponding population and sample, the research variables and relationship of variables, operational definitions, survey instruments, reliability and validity, data collection procedure, research questions with their respective hypotheses, data analysis and strategy and the limitations of the study.

The literature review supports the study of the relationship between monetary motivation, job performance and job satisfaction at multicultural for-profit institutions of higher learning.

The survey has included four sets of instruments: 1). Demographic Characteristics, 2). Money Ethic Scale (MES), 3). Job Involvement Scale (JIS) and 4). Minnesota Satisfaction Questionnaire (MSQ). Survey instruments will be collected in Zoomerang.com and exported to SPSS 12.0 for statistical analysis. The reliability and validity test, descriptive statistics, correlation analysis, internal reliability and normality are used to investigate variables in the study.

The study has two research questions and ten hypotheses that are tested and discussed in Chapter IV.

IV – ANALYSIS AND RESULTS

This chapter presents the results of analyzed data from the ten hypotheses developed in chapter III. The purpose of this study was to examine the relationship between monetary motivation, job performance and job satisfaction at multicultural for-profit institutions of higher learning. The following sections present demographics of the sample population, descriptive frequencies of the respondents, a factor analysis discussion, test of normality, reliability analysis of the instrument used and results of hypothesis tests.

Demographics of Sample Population

A survey invitation was sent to a convenience sample of 425 online students and employees at multicultural for-profit institutions of higher learning across the United States. Convenience sampling is primarily used to obtain a sample of convenient elements (Malhotra, 2007). According to Malhotra (2007) convenience sampling is inexpensive, most convenient and least time consuming when the participants are accessible, easy to measure and cooperative. A total of 207 (48.7%) participants visited the web based survey. Of those visiting the web based survey 188 (90.8%) responded within a three week time period. One hundred and sixty two (78.3%) respondents completed the survey. Twenty-six (12.6%) of the respondents were partial completes and were eliminated because the respondents did not provide answers to questions relating to satisfaction with work. The web based survey does not provide participants an opportunity to save unfinished surveys and return later to complete.

According to Couper (2000) response rates are relatively low for web surveys with email invitations when response rates can be calculated. Low response rates on the web is due primarily to outcomes at several stages in the data collection (sample members contacted by email, getting them to access the survey online and persuading sample members to complete the survey once they have started) process. If the outcome is poor at any stage the results is low response rates (Fricker, Galesic, Tourangeau and Yan, 2005). Granello and Wheaton (2004) state that unless a sampling method for the web based survey is used that allow only certain individuals access, it is impossible to know the response rates. In contrast, Deutskens, Ruyter and Wetzels (2006) found in their study of online surveys a higher response rate (28.47%) compared to mail surveys (16.58%) for companies that contacted busy and hard-to-reach professionals.

Evans and Mathur (2005) suggest the following to reduce or eliminate low response rates of web based surveys:

1. Limit the number of times respondents are contacted
2. Provide small incentives to those that respond
3. Develop best possible surveys that reduce time and effort

Online survey response rates are at best equal to other methods and sometimes worse requiring more in-depth study (Fricker and Schonlau, 2002). Variation in response rate, response speed and other methodological issues should be the focus of researchers (Sheehan and McMillan, 1999).

Descriptive Frequencies

Selected demographic variables pertaining to the respondents of this study are presented in tabular form on the following pages. Tables 7 - 12 show demographic frequencies of work and school status, age, gender, tenure and educational level.

Table 7 - Work Status Frequencies

Work Status		Frequency	Percent	Valid Percent	Cumulative Percent
	Full-time Employee	146	90.1	90.1	90.1
	Part-time Employee	10	6.2	6.2	96.3
	Not Working	6	3.7	3.7	100.0
	Total	162	100.0	100.0	

The majority of respondents for Table 7 have a work status of full-time (90.1%), followed by part-time (6.2%) and not working (3.7%), which may indicate that part-time and not working are students. Hoover's (2007) provided the For-Profit Education Industry Competitive Landscape for 2006 of four of the largest publicly traded higher learning education companies including employee count (see Table 1). Thus, this study is a convenience sample of the population and is not representative of the work-status of the for-profit higher education industry collectively.

Table 8 - School Status Frequencies

School Status	Frequency	Percent	Valid Percent	Cumulative Percent
Full-time Student	57	35.2	35.2	35.2
Part-time Student	28	17.3	17.3	52.5
Not in School	77	47.5	47.5	100.0
Total	162	100.0	100.0	

Table 8 shows school status of not in school 47%, full-time 35.2% and part-time 17.3%. The number of respondents represents 162 (100.0%) and the majority of respondents (47.5%) are not in school.

Table 9 - Age Group Frequencies

Age	Frequency	Percent	Valid Percent	Cumulative Percent
21-30	32	19.8	19.8	19.8
31-40	41	25.3	25.3	45.1
41-50	55	34.0	34.0	79.0
51-60	24	14.8	14.8	93.8
61 and above	10	6.2	6.2	100.0
Total	162	100.0	100.0	

Table 9 shows age group variation from 21 to 61 and above. Of the 162 respondents, 34.0% were between the ages of 41 and 50, 25.3% were between the ages of 31 and 40 and 19.8% were between the ages of 21-30. The most frequent age range for this group is 21-50 years, representing 79.0% of the respondents. The age range of 18-20 did not respond.

Table 10 - Gender Frequencies

Gender	Frequency	Percent	Valid Percent	Cumulative Percent
Male	48	29.6	29.6	29.6
Female	114	70.4	70.4	100.0
Total	162	100.0	100.0	

The number of respondents for Table 10 demographic frequencies of gender was 162 (100.0%). More females (70.4%) responded than males (29.6%).

Table 11 - Tenure Frequencies

Tenure	Frequency	Percent	Valid Percent	Cumulative Percent
5 or less years	79	48.8	48.8	48.8
6-15 years	52	32.1	32.1	80.9
16-25 years	19	11.7	11.7	92.6
More than 25 years	12	7.4	7.4	100.0
Total	162	100.0	100.0	

The majority of the 162 respondents in Table 11 have tenure of 5 or less years (48.8%) followed by tenure of 6-15 years (32.1%). A small percentage of respondents have more than 25 years of tenure (7.4%).

In Table 12, the educational level ranged from high school diploma/GED to masters degree or above. The majority of the respondents had a 4-year degree (44.4%), followed closely by those with a master's degree or above (38.3%). Those respondents reporting some college may be students just starting college or employees that did not finish college (15.4%). There were an insufficient number of respondents in the category of high school diploma/GED (1.9%).

Table 12 - Educational Level Frequencies

Educational Level	Frequency	%	Valid Percent	Cumulative Percent
High School Diploma/GED	3	1.9	1.9	1.9
Some College	25	15.4	15.4	17.3
4-year Degree	72	44.4	44.4	61.7
Masters Degree or Above	62	38.3	38.3	100.0
Total	162	100.0	100.0	

Factor Analysis

This section describes the confirmatory factor analysis for the following scales: Money Ethic Scale (MES), Job Involvement Scale (JIS) and Minnesota Satisfaction Questionnaire (MSQ). The factors were not used for subsequent analysis but used for comparative purposes.

Hair, Anderson, Tatham and Black (1998) state that the primary purpose of factor analysis is so that summarization and data reduction is achieved. Summarization describes data in a much smaller number of concepts than the original variables and data reduction calculates scores of dimensions then substitutes them for the original variables (Hair, et al, 1998). According to Malhotra (2007) factor analysis is an interdependence technique that examines the entire set of interdependent relationships or correlations among a set of variables.

Money Ethic Scale. The Money Ethic Scale (MES) contained 12 items and 6 dimensions in the instrument: good or positive attitudes (G), evil (E), achievement (A), respect or self-esteem (R), budget (B) and freedom or power (F). The Latent Root Criterion was used to extract factors. According to Hair, et al. the Latent Root Criterion is the most commonly used and simple to apply to principle component analysis. From the 12 item scale, four components were extracted and considered significant.

Job Involvement Scale. The Job Involvement Scale (JIS) contains 15 items. The purpose of the JIS (Lodahl & Kejner, 1965) is to measure an individual's value towards work (work involvement) and the extent that individual wants to perform well (job motivation). The Latent Root Criterion was used to extract factors. From the 9 item scale, two components were extracted and accounted for the total variance explained of the job involvement scale.

Minnesota Satisfaction Questionnaire. The Minnesota Satisfaction Questionnaire (MSQ) contained 20 items and 4 dimensions in the instrument: extrinsic, intrinsic, working conditions and co-worker job satisfaction. The Latent

Root Criterion was used to extract factors. From the 20 item scale, four components were extracted and considered significant.

Normality

A fundamental assumption for statistical analysis is that the data samples are from a population that is normal. The normal probability plot (P-Plot) was used to compare the cumulative proportions of actual data values to determine whether the distribution of a variable matches a given distribution. Based on the results of the normal probability plot (P-Plot) for normality, the Money Ethic Scale (MES), Job Involvement Scale (JIV) and Minnesota Satisfaction Questionnaire (MSQ) are accepted as coming from a normal distribution.

Reliability Analysis

The reliability of the Money Ethic Scale (MES), Job Involvement Scale (JIS) and Minnesota Satisfaction Questionnaire (MSQ) was tested for the sample population of this study using Cronbach's Coefficient Alpha. Cronbach's Coefficient Alpha (*a*) is a measure of internal reliability or consistency of the instrument that indicate how much the questions are measuring the same thing (Einstein, n.d.). The acceptable reliability as stated in Chapter III is 0.70. Each of the scales were summed and used as one scale.

The Money Ethic Scale (MES) has the lowest reliability coefficient of 0.68 with two items reverse coded (Factor Evil). Additional testing for internal reliability indicated that one item was not a good fit with the others. This one item if removed would produce a reliability coefficient of 0.72 (item 11).

Dunford, Boudreau and Boswell (2005) reported the MES 8 item scale reliability coefficient alpha of 0.85. Thozhur, Riley and Szivas (2006) reported the MES 12 item scale reliability coefficient alpha of 0.72. Vitell, Paolillo and Singh (2006) separated the scale into four separate dimensions and reported the MES 17 item scale reliability coefficient alpha as follows: important, 0.853; success, 0.823; motivator, 0.893 and rich, 0.880. Tang (1995) reported the MES 12 item scale reliability coefficient alpha of 0.70.

The reliability of the Job Involvement Scale (JIS) 0.71 and the items within are found to be reliable as demonstrated by the Cronbach's Coefficient Alpha.

Capon and Chernyshenko (2007) reported the JIS 6 item scale reliability coefficient alpha of 0.72, Kelloway, Catano and Carroll (2000) reported the JIS 6 item scale reliability coefficient alpha of 0.87 and Kuhnert and Palmer (1991) reported the JIS 3 item scale reliability coefficient alpha of 0.74. Ramsey, Lassk and Marshall (1995) reported a wide-ranging choice of the JIS 20 (0.79), 6 (0.70) and 4 (0.69) item scale reliability coefficient alpha.

The reliability of the Minnesota Satisfaction Questionnaire (MSQ) 0.92 and the items within are found to be reliable as demonstrated by the Cronbach's Coefficient Alpha.

Kinnoin (2005) reported the MSQ 20 item scale reliability coefficient alpha of 0.92 and Udechukwu (2007) reported the MSQ 20 item scale internal consistency alpha of 0.88. Table 13 provides the results of the Cronbach's Coefficient Alpha for each scale.

Table 13 - Reliability of Scales

No. of Items	Scales	Cronbach's Coefficient Alpha
12	Money Ethic Scale	0.68
9	Job Involvement Scale	0.71
20	Minnesota Satisfaction Questionnaire	0.92

Research Questions and Hypotheses

The following research questions will guide the hypotheses of this study:

- **Q1**. Is monetary motivation related to job performance at multicultural for-profit institutions of higher learning?
- **Q2**. Is monetary motivation related to job satisfaction at multicultural for-profit institutions of higher learning?

According to Baron and Kenny (1986) measuring and testing moderational hypotheses depends on the level of measurement of the independent variable and the moderator variable. As such, the moderator variable (age, gender, tenure and educational level) effect on the independent variable (monetary motivation) will be examined using regression analysis as recommended by Baron and Kenny in their research entitled *"The Moderator-Mediator Variable Distinction in Social Psychological Research: Conceptual, Strategic and Statistical Considerations."*

Age, tenure and educational level are classified as categorical variables with no value limit or simply stated these variables are divided into many groups. Gender is classified as a categorical variable with two value limit or this variable is divided into independent groups. Monetary motivation (money attitudes) the independent variable is classified as continuous variable or in other words, levels of the variable exist between the values specified (Sims, 2000).

To test the relationship effect of the moderators (age, gender, tenure and educational level) these categorical moderator variables are multiplied by the independent continuous variable monetary motivation (money attitudes). The effect of the moderator is then tested by the relationship of moderator and independent variables on the dependent variables job performance and job satisfaction by means of the General Linear Model (GLM) Univariate method.

H01: The effects of monetary motivation on job performance will decrease or have no effect with age at multicultural for-profit institutions of higher learning.

H1A: The effects of monetary motivation on job performance will increase or have no effect with age at multicultural for-profit institutions of higher learning.

The General Linear Model Univariate was performed to test null hypothesis 1. Table 14 and 15 below reveal that the effect of age on the dependent variable job performance which measures an individual's value towards work and the extent that individual wants to perform well (Cammann, Fichman, Jenkins & Klesh, 1979; Lodahl & Kejner, 1965) was not significant. None of the Beta coefficients for age are significant. The probability level of .927 is greater than the established cut-off of 0.05, so the results indicate that the null hypothesis is not rejected. Hence, age does not affect job performance and there is no support for the hypothesis that there is a correlation between monetary motivation and job performance in younger versus older student and employees at multicultural for-profit institutions of higher learning.

Table 14 - Tests of Between-Subjects Effects

Dependent Variable: Job Performance

Source	Type III Sum of Squares	df	Mean Square	F	Sig.	Partial Eta Squared
Corrected Model	398.824(b)	5	79.765	3.457	.005	.100
Intercept	1656.089	1	1656.089	71.781	.000	.315
Money Attitudes	369.240	1	369.240	16.004	.000	.093
Age	20.240	4	5.060	.219	.927	.006
Error	3599.151	156	23.071			
Total	113406.000	162				
Corrected Total	3997.975	161				

a Computed using alpha = .05
b R Squared = .100 (Adjusted R Squared = .071)

H02: The effects of monetary motivation on job satisfaction will decrease or have no affect with age at multicultural for-profit institutions of higher learning.

H2A: The effects of monetary motivation on job satisfaction will increase or have no effect with age at multicultural for-profit institutions of higher learning.

Table 15 - Univariate Tests – Age and Job Performance

Dependent Variable: Job Performance

	Sum of Squares	df	Mean Square	F	Sig.	Partial Eta Squared
Contrast	20.240	4	5.060	.219	.927	.006
Error	3599.151	156	23.071			

The F tests the effect of Age. This test is based on the linearly independent pairwise comparisons among the estimated marginal means.
a Computed using alpha = .05

Table 16 and 17 below reveal that the relationship between monetary motivation, job satisfaction and age is not significant (.707) for hypothesis 2. Also, the Parameter Estimates show none of the Beta coefficients for age as significant. Given the probability level .707 is greater than the alpha of 0.05 the null hypothesis can not be rejected. Therefore, there is no support for the hypothesis that monetary motivation on job satisfaction will increase or have no effect in younger versus older student and employees at multicultural for-profit institutions of higher learning.

Table 16 - Tests of Between-Subjects Effects

Dependent Variable: Job Satisfaction

Source	Type III Sum of Squares	df	Mean Square	F	Sig.	Partial Eta Squared
Corrected Model	551.429(b)	5	110.286	.596	.703	.019
Intercept	21751.096	1	21751.096	117.545	.000	.430
Money Attitudes	159.280	1	159.280	.861	.355	.005
Age	399.038	4	99.760	.539	.707	.014
Error	28867.071	156	185.045			
Total	827003.000	162				
Corrected Total	29418.500	161				

a Computed using alpha = .05
b R Squared = .019 (Adjusted R Squared = -.013)

H03: The effects of monetary motivation on job performance will be higher for females than males at multicultural for-profit institutions of higher learning.
H3A: The effects of monetary motivation on job performance will be lower for females than males at multicultural for-profit institutions of higher learning.

Table 17 - Univariate Tests – Age and Job Satisfaction

Dependent Variable: Job Satisfaction

	Sum of Squares	df	Mean Square	F	Sig.	Partial Eta Squared
Contrast	399.038	4	99.760	.539	.707	.014
Error	28867.071	156	185.045			

The F tests the effect of Age. This test is based on the linearly independent pairwise comparisons among the estimated marginal means.
a Computed using alpha = .05

Females in this study accounted for 70.4% (114) and males accounted for 29.6% (48) of the respondents. The General Linear Model Univariate method was performed to test if monetary motivation on job performance will be higher for females than males (null hypothesis 3). Table 18 and 19 show that the effect of gender on the dependent variable job performance was not significant. None of the Beta coefficients for gender are significant. The probability level of .806 is greater than the established cut-off of 0.05, so the results indicate that the null hypothesis is not rejected. Hence, gender does not affect job performance and there is no support for the hypothesis that there is a correlation between monetary motivation and job performance of females versus males at multicultural for-profit institutions of higher learning.

Table 18 - Tests of Between-Subjects Effects

Dependent Variable: Job Performance

Source	Type III Sum of Squares	df	Mean Square	F	Sig.	Partial Eta Squared
Corrected Model	379.959(b)	2	189.980	8.349	.000	.095
Intercept	1723.336	1	1723.336	75.735	.000	.323
Money Attitudes	360.848	1	360.848	15.858	.000	.091
Gender	1.375	1	1.375	.060	.806	.000
Error	3618.016	159	22.755			
Total	113406.000	162				
Corrected Total	3997.975	161				

a Computed using alpha = .05
b R Squared = .095 (Adjusted R Squared = .084)

H04: The effects of monetary motivation on job satisfaction will be higher for males than females at multicultural for-profit institutions of higher learning.

H4A: The effects of monetary motivation on job satisfaction will be lower for males than females at multicultural for-profit institutions of higher learning.

Table 19 - Univariate Tests – Gender and Job Performance

Dependent Variable: Job Performance

	Sum of Squares	df	Mean Square	F	Sig.	Partial Eta Squared
Contrast	1.375	1	1.375	.060	.806	.000
Error	3618.016	159	22.755			

The F tests the effect of Gender. This test is based on the linearly independent pairwise comparisons among the estimated marginal means.
a Computed using alpha = .05

The General Linear Model Univariate method was performed to test if monetary motivation on job satisfaction will be higher for males than females (null hypothesis 4). Table 20 and 21 show that the effect of gender on the dependent variable job satisfaction was not significant. None of the Beta coefficients for gender are significant. The probability level of .776 is greater than the established cut-off of 0.05, so the results indicate that the null hypothesis is not rejected. Hence, gender does not affect job satisfaction and there is no support for the hypothesis that monetary motivation on job satisfaction will be lower for males versus females at multicultural for-profit institutions of higher learning.

Table 20 - Tests of Between-Subjects Effects

Dependent Variable: Job Satisfaction

Source	Type III Sum of Squares	df	Mean Square	F	Sig.	Partial Eta Squared
Corrected Model	167.317(b)	2	83.658	.455	.635	.006
Intercept	22957.887	1	22957.887	124.792	.000	.440
Money Attitudes	133.093	1	133.093	.723	.396	.005
Gender	14.926	1	14.926	.081	.776	.001
Error	29251.183	159	183.970			
Total	827003.000	162				
Corrected Total	29418.500	161				

a Computed using alpha = .05
b R Squared = .006 (Adjusted R Squared = -.007)

Table 21 - Univariate Tests – Gender and Job Satisfaction

Dependent Variable: Job Satisfaction

	Sum of Squares	df	Mean Square	F	Sig.	Partial Eta Squared
Contrast	14.926	1	14.926	.081	.776	.001
Error	29251.183	159	183.970			

The F tests the effect of Gender. This test is based on the linearly independent pairwise comparisons among the estimated marginal means.
a Computed using alpha = .05

H05: The effects of monetary motivation on job performance will increase with tenure at multicultural for-profit institutions of higher learning.

H5A: The effects of monetary motivation on job performance will decrease with tenure at multicultural for-profit institutions of higher learning.

The majority of the 162 respondents in this study have tenure of 5 or less years (48.8%). The General Linear Model Univariate was performed to test null hypothesis 5. Table 22 and 23 below reveal that the effect of tenure on the dependent variable job performance was not significant. None of the Beta coefficients for tenure are significant. The probability level of .229 is greater than the established cut-off of 0.05, so the results indicate that the null hypothesis is not rejected. Hence, tenure does not affect job performance and there is no support for the hypothesis that there is a correlation between monetary motivation, job performance and tenure at multicultural for-profit institutions of higher learning.

Table 22 - Tests of Between-Subjects Effects

Dependent Variable: Job Performance

Source	Type III Sum of Squares	df	Mean Square	F	Sig.	Partial Eta Squared
Corrected Model	476.473(b)	4	119.118	5.311	.000	.119
Intercept	1589.755	1	1589.755	70.876	.000	.311
Money Attitudes	383.196	1	383.196	17.084	.000	.098
Tenure	97.889	3	32.630	1.455	.229	.027
Error	3521.502	157	22.430			
Total	113406.000	162				
Corrected Total	3997.975	161				

a Computed using alpha = .05
b R Squared = .119 (Adjusted R Squared = .097)

Table 23 - Univariate Tests – Tenure and Job Performance

Dependent Variable: Job Performance

	Sum of Squares	df	Mean Square	F	Sig.	Partial Eta Squared
Contrast	97.889	3	32.630	1.455	.229	.027
Error	3521.502	157	22.430			

The F tests the effect of Tenure. This test is based on the linearly independent pairwise comparisons among the estimated marginal means.
a Computed using alpha = .05

H06: The effects of monetary motivation on job satisfaction will increase with tenure at multicultural for-profit institutions of higher learning.

H6A: The effects of monetary motivation on job satisfaction will decrease with tenure at multicultural for-profit institutions of higher learning.

The General Linear Model Univariate was performed to test null hypothesis 6. Table 24 and 25 below show that the effect of tenure on the dependent variable job satisfaction was not significant. None of the Beta coefficients for tenure are significant. The probability level of .528 is greater than the established cut-off of 0.05, so the results indicate that the null hypothesis is not rejected. Hence, tenure does not affect job satisfaction and there is no support for the hypothesis that monetary motivation on job satisfaction will decrease with tenure at multicultural for-profit institutions of higher learning.

Table 24 - Tests of Between-Subjects Effects

Dependent Variable: Job Satisfaction

Source	Type III Sum of Squares	df	Mean Square	F	Sig.	Partial Eta Squared
Corrected Model	562.348(b)	4	140.587	.765	.550	.019
Intercept	23269.682	1	23269.682	126.61	.000	.446
Money Attitudes	120.702	1	120.702	.657	.419	.004
Tenure	409.957	3	136.652	.743	.528	.014
Error	28856.152	157	183.797			
Total	827003.000	162				
Corrected Total	29418.500	161				

a Computed using alpha = .05
b R Squared = .019 (Adjusted R Squared = -.006)

Table 25 - Univariate Tests – Tenure and Job Satisfaction

Dependent Variable: Job Satisfaction

	Sum of Squares	df	Mean Square	F	Sig.	Partial Eta Squared
Contrast	409.957	3	136.652	.743	.528	.014
Error	28856.152	157	183.797			

The F tests the effect of Tenure. This test is based on the linearly independent pairwise comparisons among the estimated marginal means.
a Computed using alpha = .05

H07: The effects of monetary motivation on job performance will increase with educational level of the employee at multicultural for-profit institutions of higher learning.

H7A: The effects of monetary motivation on job performance will decrease with educational level of the employee at multicultural for-profit institutions of higher learning.

Table 26 - Tests of Between-Subjects Effects

Dependent Variable: Job Performance

Source	Type III Sum of Squares	df	Mean Square	F	Sig.	Partial Eta Squared
Corrected Model	410.815(b)	4	102.704	4.495	.002	.103
Intercept	1355.042	1	1355.042	59.306	.000	.274
Money Attitudes	349.199	1	349.199	15.283	.000	.089
Educational Level	32.230	3	10.743	.470	.703	.009
Error	3587.161	157	22.848			
Total	113406.000	162				
Corrected Total	3997.975	161				

a Computed using alpha = .05
b R Squared = .103 (Adjusted R Squared = .080)

The educational level of respondents in this study ranged from high school diploma/GED to masters degree or above. The majority of the respondents had a 4-year degree (44.4%), followed closely by those with a master's degree or above (38.3%). Table 26 and 27 below reveal that the relationship between monetary motivation, job performance and educational level is not significant (.703) for hypothesis 7. Also, the Parameter Estimates show none of the Beta coefficients for educational level as significant. Given the probability level .703 is greater than the alpha of 0.05 the null hypothesis cannot be rejected. Therefore, there is no support for the hypothesis that there is a correlation between monetary motivation and job performance in educational level at multicultural for-profit institutions of higher learning.

Table 27 - Univariate Tests – Educational Level and Job Performance

Dependent Variable: Job Performance

	Sum of Squares	df	Mean Square	F	Sig.	Partial Eta Squared
Contrast	32.230	3	10.743	.470	.703	.009
Error	3587.161	157	22.848			

The F tests the effect of Q 6: 6. Educational Level. This test is based on the linearly independent pairwise comparisons among the estimated marginal means.
a Computed using alpha = .05

H08: The effects of monetary motivation on job satisfaction will increase with educational level at multicultural for-profit institutions of higher learning.
H8A: The effects of monetary motivation on job satisfaction will decrease with educational level at multicultural for-profit institutions of higher learning.

Table 28 - Tests of Between-Subjects Effects

Dependent Variable: Job Satisfaction

Source	Type III Sum of Squares	df	Mean Square	F	Sig.	Partial Eta Squared
Corrected Model	596.687(b)	4	149.172	.813	.519	.020
Intercept	19825.499	1	19825.499	107.995	.000	.408
Money Attitudes	47.871	1	47.871	.261	.610	.002
Educational Level	444.296	3	148.099	.807	.492	.015
Error	28821.813	157	183.578			
Total	827003.000	162				
Corrected Total	29418.500	161				

a Computed using alpha = .05
b R Squared = .020 (Adjusted R Squared = -.005)

The General Linear Model Univariate was performed to test null hypothesis 8. The General Linear Model Univariate was performed to test null hypothesis 6. Table 28 and 29 below show that the effect of educational level on the dependent variable job satisfaction was not significant. None of the Beta coefficients for educational level are significant. The probability level of .492 is greater than the established cut-off of 0.05, so the results indicate that the null hypothesis is not rejected. Hence, educational level does not affect job satisfaction and there is no support for the hypothesis that monetary motivation on job satisfaction will decrease with educational level at multicultural for-profit institutions of higher learning.

Table 29 - Univariate Tests – Educational Level and Job Satisfaction

Dependent Variable: Job Satisfaction

	Sum of Squares	df	Mean Square	F	Sig.	Partial Eta Squared
Contrast	444.296	3	148.099	.807	.492	.015
Error	28821.813	157	183.578			

The F tests the effect of Q 6: 6. Educational Level. This test is based on the linearly independent pairwise comparisons among the estimated marginal means.
a Computed using alpha = .05

H09: The effects of monetary motivation on job performance will increase at multicultural for-profit institutions of higher learning.
H9A: The effects of monetary motivation on job performance will decrease at multicultural for-profit institutions of higher learning.

The General Linear Model Univariate test was used. Table 30 below shows that the effect of the dependent variable job performance on the independent variable monetary motivation is significant (.000). The probability level of .000 is less than the established cut-off of 0.05, so the results indicate that the null hypothesis is rejected. Thus, the effects of monetary motivation on job performance will increase at multicultural for-profit institutions of higher learning is not supported. Hence, there is support for the hypothesis that monetary motivation on job performance will decrease at multicultural for-profit institutions of higher learning.

H10: The effects of monetary motivation on job satisfaction will increase at multicultural for-profit institutions of higher learning.
H10A: The effects of monetary motivation on job satisfaction will decrease at multicultural for-profit institutions of higher learning.

The General Linear Model Univariate test was used. Table 31 below shows that the effect of the dependent variable job satisfaction on the independent variable monetary motivation is not significant (.363). The probability level of .363 is greater than the established cut-off of 0.05, so the results indicate that the null hypothesis is accepted. Thus, the effects of monetary motivation on job satisfaction will increase at multicultural for-profit institutions of higher learning is supported. Hence, there is no support for the hypothesis that monetary motivation on job satisfaction will decrease at multicultural for-profit institutions of higher learning.

Table 30 - Tests of Between-Subjects Effects

Dependent Variable: Job Performance

Source	Type III Sum of Squares	df	Mean Square	F	Sig.	Partial Eta Squared
Corrected Model	378.584(b)	1	378.584	16.736	.000	.095
Intercept	1726.870	1	1726.870	76.339	.000	.323
Money Attitudes	378.584	1	378.584	16.736	.000	.095
Error	3619.391	160	22.621			
Total	113406.000	162				
Corrected Total	3997.975	161				

a Computed using alpha = .05
b R Squared = .095 (Adjusted R Squared = .089)

Table 31 - Tests of Between-Subjects Effects

Dependent Variable: Job Satisfaction

Source	Type III Sum of Squares	df	Mean Square	F	Sig.	Partial Eta Squared
Corrected Model	152.391(b)	1	152.391	.833	.363	.005
Intercept	23015.298	1	23015.298	125.826	.000	.440
Money Attitudes	152.391	1	152.391	.833	.363	.005
Error	29266.109	160	182.913			
Total	827003.000	162				
Corrected Total	29418.500	161				

a Computed using alpha = .05
b R Squared = .005 (Adjusted R Squared = -.001)

Table 32 - Results of Hypothesis Tests

Hypo. #	Null Hypotheses	Results
H1	*The effects of monetary motivation on job performance will decrease or have no effect with age at multicultural for-profit institutions of higher learning.*	Failed to reject the null
H2	*The effects of monetary motivation on job satisfaction will decrease or have no affect with age at multicultural for-profit institutions of higher learning.*	Failed to reject the null
H3	*The effects of monetary motivation on job performance will be higher for females than males at multicultural for-profit institutions of higher learning.*	Failed to reject the null
H4	*The effects of monetary motivation on job satisfaction will be higher for males than females at multicultural for-profit institutions of higher learning.*	Failed to reject the null
H5	*The effects of monetary motivation on job performance will increase with tenure at multicultural for-profit institutions of higher learning.*	Failed to reject the null
H6	*The effects of monetary motivation on job satisfaction will increase with tenure at multicultural for-profit institutions of higher learning.*	Failed to reject the null
H7	*The effects of monetary motivation on job performance will increase with educational level of the employee at multicultural for-profit institutions of higher learning.*	Failed to reject the null
H8	*The effects of monetary motivation on job satisfaction will increase with educational level at multicultural for-profit institutions of higher learning.*	Failed to reject the null
H9	*The effects of monetary motivation on job performance will increase at multicultural for-profit institutions of higher learning.*	Failed to accept the null
H10	*The effects of monetary motivation on job satisfaction will increase at multicultural for-profit institutions of higher learning.*	Failed to reject the null

Summary of Results

The results were analyzed from the responses of 162 online students and employees at multicultural for profit institutions of higher learning across the United States. This chapter began with a presentation of demographics of the sample population, descriptive frequencies, factor analysis, normality, reliability analysis, research questions and finally a discussion of hypothesis. The research used regression analysis to test the instruments and hypotheses. Table 32 summarizes the results of testing for the ten hypotheses.

The study to summarize and discuss the findings, implication of the findings, research contributions, research limitation, recommendation for future research and the final conclusion are discussed in Chapter 5.

CHAPTER FIVE

V - CONCLUSIONS

This chapter presents the summary, recommendations and conclusions for this research developed from chapters I – IV. The study revealed several interesting findings about the relationship of monetary motivation, job performance and job satisfaction at multicultural for-profit institutions of higher learning. The following sections presents the objectives of the study, research questions and review of related literature, research methodology, summary of research findings, practical implications, limitations of the study, recommendations for future research and conclusion.

Summary, Recommendations & Conclusions

The purpose of this study was to determine if there were relationships among monetary motivation, job performance and job satisfaction at multicultural for-profit institutions of higher learning. Comparisons among age, gender, tenure and educational level were examined. The results of this research can provide better understanding of the variables proposed and can refer to other organizations, specifically the non-profit industry of higher learning, which is also undergoing organizational changes with respect to employee and student attraction, retention and motivation.

The purpose of this research was to investigate the relationship between the three variables monetary motivation, job performance and job satisfaction in the for-profit higher education industry. However, the researcher found no literature that examined these three variables with the Money Ethic Scale (MES), Job Involvement Scale (JIS) and Minnesota Satisfaction Questionnaire (MSQ). As recently as 1999, Furnham and Okamura stated that little research had been conducted on money due to the neglected and under-researched topic in psychometric instruments to measure monetary beliefs and behaviors (Medina, Saegert and Gresham, 1996). Kinser and Levy (2005) in their study *"The For-Profit Sector: U.S. Patterns and International Echoes in Higher Education"* state that the availability of information is quite limited on the for-profit higher education sector as researchers only recently are studying its scope and impact. However, research on both job performance and job satisfaction is extensively researched throughout the business literature. Independently, some of the previous research in these areas could be replicated. This study was organized around two research questions:

Q1. Is monetary motivation related to job performance?

We all know that decisions about compensation are important. As these decisions about compensation in essences help determine organizational culture, reward systems and employee behavior. Pfeffer (1988) in his article *"Six Dangerous Myths About Pay"* states that business people are adopting misleading and incorrect notions about how to pay people and why. Two myths that are directly related to this study are:

Myth # 5: Individual incentive pay improves performance.

According to Pfeffer (1988) both the individual and the organization performance is undermined with individual incentive pay. Several studies suggest that individual incentives has a negative impact on teamwork, encourages short-term focus and leads people to believe that pay is not related to performance. The first research question is supported by the findings of previous researchers as money did not motivate any age group's performance and may in-fact decrease performance of some individuals in this study. The results generated in this study were more in agreement with several researchers who provided strong evidence that pay is a powerful motivator of performance if pay is noticeable contingent on performance (Bishop, 1987; Gerhart & Milkovich, 1992; Jenkins, Mitra, Gupta & Shaw, 1998; Rynes et al., 2004).

Myth # 6: People work primarily for money.

People work more for meaning in their lives not just for money. In reality, they work to have fun. Companies that are not aware or ignore this reality will pay the price in lack of loyalty and commitment (Pfeffer, 1988). In agreement with Pfeffer, Vroom (1964) states that the majority of individuals worked for reasons that had nothing to do with money. Individuals want to obtain skills, acceptance, respect and the opportunity to contribute to society and money was just a necessary part of the work-motivation relationship. Russell (1930) argued that the purpose of work is essential for happiness. Kovack (1987) points out that a company would be in a better position to stimulate employees to perform well, if that company knew what drove employees to work. The key, however, is that managers avoid the assumption that what motivates them also motivates their employees as well (Wessler, 1984).

Q2. Is monetary motivation related to job satisfaction?

Satisfaction with one's pay has a direct affect on whether the employee feels valued within the organization. A person with job satisfaction holds a positive attitude about the job, as opposed to a person who is dissatisfied with his or her job (Milbourn & Haight, 2004). According to Saari and Judge (2004) a good match between employees and jobs will ensure people are placed into appropriate jobs, thus enhancing job satisfaction.

According to Tang (2006) a contributor to low job satisfaction is low pay satisfaction because job satisfaction consists of satisfaction with work, pay, promotions, supervision and coworkers. However, Kauffman (1987) writes that older workers are motivated by intrinsic rewards such as a pat on the back. Pay and promotions appear to be less important for older workers (Bourne, 1982). Tang (1992) writes in his study that money attitudes of young adults are influenced by their age – money seen as evil.

The second research question is supported by the findings of Bourne, Kauffman and Tang as money did not motivate any age group's job satisfaction. The results generated in this study were more in agreement with researchers who provided strong evidence that monetary motivation is related to job satisfaction and include: Allen and Velden (2001) state that job satisfaction is influenced by wages and skill match, Bedeian et al (1992) wrote that tenure is a better predictor of job satisfaction than age, Lawler (1971) in his research wrote that the smaller the difference between what is expected and the actual pay received the higher the level of job satisfaction and Tang and Talpade (1999) in their study wrote that males have higher satisfaction with pay than females.

Research Methodology

Out of 425 online survey invitations sent to a convenience sample, 162 were completed. Online students and employees at various multicultural for-profit institutions of higher learning participated across the United States. Data on money attitude, job performance and job satisfaction was gathered using validated surveys. The data was analyzed using the Statistical Product and Service Solutions (SPSS) formally known as Statistical Package for Social Sciences version 12.0.

Summary of Findings

The findings reported in this study are based on a web based administered survey to a convenience sampled population of employees and students at various for-profit higher learning institutions across the United States.

Reliability for the sample population was tested using Cronbach's Coefficient Alpha. Cronbach's Coefficient Alpha (*a*) is a measure of internal reliability or consistency of the instrument that indicates how much the questions are measuring the same thing (Einstein, n.d.). Cronbach's Alpha coefficients for this study show that reliability was appropriate for the Job Involvement Scale (JIS) at 0.71 and the Minnesota Satisfaction Questionnaire (MSQ) at 0.92. The Money Ethic Scale (MES) had the lowest reliability coefficient of 0.68. Additional testing for internal reliability indicated that one item was not a good fit with the others. This one item if removed would produce a reliability coefficient of 0.72 (item 11).

Regression Analysis showed that none of the Beta coefficients for age, gender, tenure and educational level are significant. The effects of the independent variable monetary motivation on the dependent variables job performance and job satisfaction with moderator variables age, gender, tenure and educational level are not statistically significant. Hypotheses 9 has significance (.000) well below the alpha < 0.05 standard.

The results of the study indicate that for the null hypotheses, that the effects of monetary motivation on job performance and job satisfaction at multicultural for-profit institutions of higher learning must be accepted for the facets of age, gender, tenure and educational level.

Hypotheses 1 and 2. Hypotheses 1 and 2 in this study examined the relationship between monetary motivation and the dependent variables job performance and job satisfaction and moderator variable age. Strong empirical analysis resulted in the acceptance of null hypothesis 1 and 2. In Hypothesis 1 the probability level of .927 is greater than the established cut-off of 0.05; thus money will not motivate any age group's performance as supported by researchers in the area of age and job performance (McEvoy & Cascio, 1989; Waldman & Avolio, 1986). For Hypothesis 2 given the probability level .707 is greater than the alpha of 0.05; money will not motivate any age group's job satisfaction as supported by researchers Tu, Plaisent, Bernard and Maguiraga (2005).

Hypotheses 3 and 4. Hypotheses 3 and 4 in this study examined the relationship between monetary motivation and the dependent variables job performance and job satisfaction and the moderator variable gender. Strong empirical analysis resulted in the acceptance of null hypothesis 3 and 4. For Hypothesis 3 the probability level of .806 is greater than the established cut-off of 0.05; money motivation on job performance is higher for females versus males as supported by researchers in the area gender and job performance (Tang et al., 2006; Taynor & Deaux, 1973, 1975). In Hypotheses 4 given the probability level of .776 is greater than the alpha of 0.05; money as a motivator on job satisfaction is higher for males versus females as supported by researchers in the area of job satisfaction and gender (Okpara et al., 2004; Tang & Talpade, 1999).

Hypotheses 5 and 6. Hypotheses 5 and 6 in this study examined the relationship between monetary motivation and the dependent variables job performance and job satisfaction and the moderator variable tenure. Strong empirical analysis resulted in the acceptance of null hypothesis 5 and 6. In Hypothesis 5 the probability level of .229 is greater than the established cut-off of 0.05; thus money motivates job performance as tenure increases is supported by researchers in the area of tenure and job performance (August et al., 2006; Barron, 2003). For Hypothesis 6 given the probability level of .528 is greater than the alpha of 0.05; money motivates job satisfaction as tenure increases is supported by researchers Bedeian et al., (1992) and Monk (2007).

Hypotheses 7 and 8. Hypotheses 7 and 8 in this study examined the relationship between monetary motivation and the dependent variables job performance and job satisfaction and the moderator variable educational level. Strong empirical analysis resulted in the acceptance of null hypothesis 7 and 8. In Hypothesis 7 the relationship between monetary motivation, job performance and educational level is not significant (.703); thus money as a motivator on job performance increases with educational level (Truxillo et al., 1998; Wise, 1975). For Hypothesis 8 the relationship between monetary motivation, job satisfaction and educational level is not significant (.492); thus money as a motivator on job satisfaction increases with educational level (Allen & Velden, 2001; Gray & Chapman, 1999).

Hypotheses 9. Hypotheses 9 in this study examined the relationship between monetary motivation and the dependent variable job performance. Strong empirical analysis resulted in the rejection of null hypothesis 9. In Hypothesis 9 the probability level of .000 is well below the alpha < 0.05 standard; thus money as a motivator decreases job performance. Monetary motivation does not have an effect on job performance; in essence money is not a motivator but may even result in lowering job performance (Lawler & Worley, 2006; Terpstra & Honoree, 2005).

Hypotheses 10. Hypotheses 10 in this study examined the relationship between monetary motivation and the dependent variable job satisfaction. Strong empirical analysis resulted in the acceptance of the null hypothesis 10. For Hypothesis 10 the probability level of .363 is greater than the established cut-off of 0.05; as such money as a motivator increases job satisfaction (Ross & Zander, 1957; Tang, 2006).

Implications for Human Resource Practitioners

The body of literature that focuses on monetary motivation in for-profit institutions of higher learning is very limited. The results of this study will add to this body of knowledge.

Several practical implications of this study exist for Human Resource (HR) Practitioners both in the for-profit and non-profit areas of higher education. First, this study does not demonstrate that monetary motivation will have an effect on any age group. As such, HR Practitioners should consider alternative methods of rewards that engage all employees to increase performance and satisfaction. One such suggested method is performance contingent pay. This scenario may eventually lead to greater effort, attraction of more able workers, reduction in losing best performers and satisfaction (Bishop, 1987). Second, this study does provide support that a relationship exists between monetary motivation and job performance for females. Previous research has shown that females seek other females as pay references to lessen the frustration comparison that would be the case when making cross-gender pay comparisons. By choosing same gender pay references, women are more likely to maintain perceptions of pay equity rather than pay parity with males (Balkin & Gomez-Mejia, 2002). HR Practitioners may have to address performance efforts of females as compared to male employees to better gauge pay parity. Third, this study does provide additional support that a relationship exists between monetary motivation and job satisfaction for males. Tang and Talpade (1999) in their study provide HR Practitioners with the necessary empirical evidence regarding the importance of employee needs and specifically that men may value money more highly than females. Fourth, this study also demonstrates that money motivates both job performance and job satisfaction as tenure increases. Research studies are in support of this current study and state that the primary purpose of tenure is to assess job performance (Barron, 2003) and that tenure is a better predictor of job satisfaction (Bedeian et al, 1992). HR practitioners must find ways to include monetary rewards as a means to better link employee job performance and job satisfaction to tenure systems. Fifth, this study does demonstrate that money as a motivator on job performance and job satisfaction increases with educational level. HR Practitioners should review their tuition reimbursement and training plan as part their overall HR planning process as a means to attract, retain and motivate existing and future employee development. Sixth, this study does not demonstrate that money as a motivator increases job performance in the for-profit institutions of higher learning but decreases job performance. This finding supports other researchers who provide evidence that pay has a direct effect on performance (Gneezy & Rustichini, 2000; Hechler & Wiener, 1974). HR Practitioners can use the findings of this study and others to review additional policies and procedures that lend themselves to appropriate use of money as an incentive to increase performance. A final implication for HR Practitioners is this study does demonstrate that money as a motivator increases job satisfaction at for-profit institutions of higher learning. According to Tang (2006) a contributor to low job satisfaction is low pay satisfaction because job satisfaction consists of satisfaction with work, pay, promotions, supervision and coworkers. The HR Practitioners role in this instance is to understand how dissatisfaction with one's work environment and compensation can lead employees into the arms of the competitor. To counteract dissatisfaction HR Practitioners should recognize that job satisfaction is indeed important and must be maintained to retain valued top performers.

HR Practitioners must continue to look for ways to play an important role in organizational strategic planning. Increased performance, productivity and job satisfaction are at a premium in today's lean and mean global economic environment. A study of this kind can be a good starting point while formulating incentive plans to retain and attract the organizations' human resources. HR Practitioners must understand that, while outsourcing or downsizing may be a way to reduce costs in certain areas of the business the remaining key employees need attractive extrinsic and intrinsic rewards to stay put on their jobs and allay their fears of here today and gone tomorrow.

Limitations of this Study

There are several limitations in this study. First, few instruments exist to properly measure money attitude. Second, survey participants may not understand the complete scope of the research and their responses may not reflect their current job situation in its entirety. During data analysis and results examination, it became apparent that the convenience sample needed a closer look. Some questions in the survey appeared to have posted a challenge to the subjects in the matter of understanding the questions. This was apparent in two questions (questions 11 and 12) on the Money Ethics Scale. While the older subjects were able to relate and answer the question about money, the younger subjects appeared to have or did not understand the question as supported by Tang's (1992) study that money attitudes of young adults are influenced by their age – money seen as evil. This issue could be considered as a deficiency or a limitation that future researchers may have to investigate further. Third, this study takes place in the for-profit higher learning industry and is limited to employees and students from a convenience sample and may not adequately represent the for-profit industry in general. It is quite obvious that the size of the sample had limitations on the findings. Several for-profit higher learning institutions were approached about participating in the study and either declined the invitation or did not respond. Fourth, the size of the institutions selected in the proposed study may influence results. Fifth, the employees' level of supervision and influence in decision making may not be representative of what was presented in the study. Finally, there was a higher percentage of females (70.4%) than males (29.6%) who participated in the study which may have skewed the results.

Recommendation for Future Research

Future research on monetary motivation, job performance and job satisfaction in the for-profit higher learning environment is needed because of the important role rewards play in attracting, motivating and retaining valued employees and students to meet organization specific long and short-term goals. Tang (2006) states to attract, retain, and motivate employees around the world an understanding is needed of the importance of money. In the for-profit higher learning industry, attitudes about money, performance and satisfaction are important as these institutions deal with the challenges associated with the need for increased revenue, stiff competition and the global economic environment.

This research study involved a convenience sample of employees and students from across the United States. There is an opportunity to expand this research if for-profit higher learning institutions are willing to openly embrace newness and provide information that is transparent particularly in the areas of compensation. Further research is definitely needed in the for-profit higher learning industry with a larger sample size to add validation and support of this study. Opportunities also exist to examine potential outcomes in the non-profit higher learning institutions. There is an opportunity to study potential differences in management and subordinates in the for-profit and non-profit areas. An additional opportunity exists in conducting studies of human resource practitioners at for-profit and non-profit higher learning institutions and the exit interview responses of both voluntary and involuntary leavers. HR Practitioners will gain validation that contribute to their HR Planning initiatives as more research is conducted in these three areas of money motivation, job performance and job satisfaction.

Conclusion

The current study was designed to establish if monetary motivation in multicultural for-profit institutions of higher learning would increase job performance and job satisfaction. This study revealed several interesting findings about the for-profit institutions of higher learning:

1. Money will not motivate any age group to increase job performance or job satisfaction.
2. Money motivation on job performance is higher for females; however, job satisfaction is higher for males.
3. Money motivates job performance and job satisfaction as tenure increases.
4. Money as a motivator on job performance and job satisfaction increases with educational level.
5. Money as a motivator decreases job performance.
6. Money as a motivator increases job satisfaction.

Students are often asked in Human Resource, Business and Organizational Behavior courses "Is money a motivator?" The answers vary according to the age, gender, tenure at place of employment, current work status and educational level of the student. Regardless of the individuals answer, we do know that the lack of money de-motivates performance and can lead to job dissatisfaction. For-profit higher educational institutions and HR Practitioners within these organizations have a strong need to understand what motivates individuals to remain competitive. Human resources within these institutions with the appropriate knowledge, skills, abilities and other characteristics (KSAOC's) can assist the for-profit higher education industry to retain their competitive advantage as the competences of that institution cannot be duplicated. However, as the higher education industry continues to increase revenue, become more competitive and global the need to reward individuals and meet stated organizational objectives is at the forefront of discussion. What attracts, motivates and retains valued students, faculty and staff? Is money the answer?

Attitudes toward money, job performance and job satisfaction in this research study may be a result of the current economic conditions. Employees and students may look at their current pay as inadequate and diminishing to cope with the ever increasing cost of goods and services. More money or substantial pay increases may be needed to entice employees to do more to increase their performance and hence be satisfied during these current turbulent economic times. Only time will tell if "Money actually makes the world go round" in multicultural for-profit higher learning institutions.

BIBLIOGRAPHY

VI - References

Alexander, M. A. (2004). Job satisfaction and organizational commitment in the local church: A study of African American male ministers (Doctoral dissertation, Nova Southeastern University – Huizenga Graduate School of Business and Entrepreneurship, 2004). *Dissertation Abstracts International, 65 (01)*. (UMI No.3119761).

Alkadry, M. G., & Tower, L.E. (2006). Unequal pay: The role of gender. *Public Administration Review, 66 (6)*, 888 – 898.

Allen, J., & Velden, R. V. (2001). Educational mismatches versus skills mismatches; effects on wages, job satisfaction, and on-the-job search. *Oxford Economic Paper, 53 (3)*, 434-452.

American Federation of Labour Unions (AFL-CIO), Retrieved April 27, 2006, from http://www.aflcio.org.

August, L., Hollenshead, C., Miller, J., & Waltman, J. (2006). Non tenure track faculty: The landscape at U.S. institutions of higher education. Center for the Education of Women, Retrieved October 27, 2007 from http://www.ceu.umich.edu.

Avery, R. D., Bouchard, T. J., Segal, N. L., & Abraham, L. M. (1989). Job satisfaction: Environmental and genetic components. *Journal of Applied Psychology, 74*, 187-192.

Babcock, P. (2005, April). Find what workers want. *HR Magazine, 50 (4)*, 51-56.

Balkin, D. B., & Gomez-Mejia, L. R. (2002). Explaining the gender effects on faculty pay increases: Do the squeaky wheels get the grease? *Group & Organization Management, 27*, 352 - 373.

Barclay, L. A., & York, K. M. (2003). Clear logic and fuzzy guidance: A policy capturing study of merit raise decisions. *Public Personnel Management, 32*, 287-299.

Barnett, R. C., & Rivers, C. (2004). Men are from earth, and so are women. It's faculty research that sets them apart. *The Chronicle of Higher Education, 51 (2)*, B11.

Barnett, T., & Schubert, E. (2002). Perceptions of the ethical work climate and covenantal relationships. *Journal of Business Ethics, 36*, 279-290.

Barron, R. M., & Kenny, D. A. (1986). The moderator-mediator variable distinction in social psychological research: Conceptual, strategic, and statistical considerations. *Journal of Personality and Social Psychology, 6*, 1173-1182.

Barron, D. (2003). Life after tenure. *The Chronicle of Higher Education, 49 (46)*, C3.

Bates, S. (2004). I love my job: How to energize disengaged employees. *HR Magazine, 49 (2)*, 44 – 51.

Bedeian, A. G., Ferris, G. R & Kacmar, K. M. (1992). Age, tenure, and job satisfaction: A tale of two perspectives. *Journal of Vocational Behavior, 40*, 33-48.

Benjamin, E. (2001). Uncertain times. *Academe, 87*, 1-35.

Benabou, R., & Tirole, J. (2003). Intrinsic and extrinsic motivation. *The Review of Economic Studies, 70*, 489-514.

Bender, K. A., Donohue, S. M., & Heywood, J. S. (2005). Job satisfaction and gender segregation. *Oxford Economic Papers, 57*, 479 - 496.

Bilimoria, D., Perry, S. R., Liang, X., Stroller, E. P., Higgins, P., & Taylor, C. (2006). How do female and male faculty members construct job satisfaction? The roles of perceived institutional leadership and mentoring and their mediating process. *Journal of Technology Transfer, 31*, 355-365.

Bishop, J. (1987). The recognition and reward of employee performance. *Journal of Labour Economics, 5*, 36 - 53.

Blumenstyk, G. (2005a). For-profit education: Online courses fuel growth. *The Chronicle of Higher Education, 51 (18)*, A11.

Blumenstyk, G. (2005b). For-profit outlook. *The Chronicle of Higher Education, 52 (14)*, A14.

Blumenstyk, G. (2006a). Why for-profit colleges are like health clubs. *The Chronicle of Higher Education, 52 (35)*, A35.

Blumenstyk, G. (2007a). Career colleges release first economic-impact study. *The Chronicle of Higher Education, 53 (44)*, A22.

Blumenstyk, G. (2007b). The chronicle index of for-profit higher education. *The Chronicle of Higher Education, 53 (23)*, A25.

Blumenstyk, G. (2007c). The chronicle index of for-profit higher education. *The Chronicle of Higher Education, 53 (36)*, A40.

Bloom, M. (1999). The performance effects of pay dispersion on individuals and organizations. *Academy of Management Journal, 42*, 25-40.

Bloom, M. (2004). The ethics of compensation systems. *Journal of Business Ethics, 52*, 149.

Bourne, B. (1982). Effect of aging on work satisfaction, performance and motivation. *Aging and Work, 5 (1)*, 37-43.

Bradt, J. A. (1996). Pay employees for their contributions. *Personnel Journal, 75*, 3-7.

Brand, M. (1999). Why tenure is indispensable. *The Chronicle of Higher Education, 45 (30)*, A64.

Bretz, R. D., & Thomas, S. L. (1992). Perceived equity, motivation and final-offer arbitration in major league baseball. *Journal of Applied Psychology, 77*, 280-287.

Brief, A. (1998). *Attitudes in and around organizations,* California: SAGE Publications, Inc.

Buhler, P. (1989). Rewards in the Organization. *Supervision,* 5 -7.

Cammann, C., Fichman, M., Jenkins, D., & Klesh, J. (1979). *The Michigan Organization Assessment Questionnaire.* Unpublished manuscript, Ann Arbor.

Canen, A. G., & Canen, A. (2001). Looking at multiculturalism in international logistics: An experiment in a higher education institution. *The International Journal of Education Management, 15 (3)*, 145-153.

Capon, J., & Chernyshenko, O.S. (2007). Applicability of civilian retention theory in the New Zealand military. *New Zealand Journal of Psychology, 36 (1)*, 50-56.

Capstone Encyclopaedia of Business (2003). Retrieved 08 October 2006, from xreferplus. http://0-www.xreferplus.com.novacat.nova.edu:80/entry/5862136.

Cascio, W. F., & Aguinis, H. (2005). *Applied psychology in human resource management,* (6th ed.) Upper Saddle River, N. J: Pearson Prentice Hall.

Champoux, J. E. (1978). A serendipitous field experiment in job design. *Journal of Vocational Behavior, 12,* 364-370.

Chan, L. (2007). Do the leaders' motivating language approaches relate to the subordinates' level of job satisfaction in a unionized work environment? (Doctoral dissertation, Nova Southeastern University – Huizenga School of Business and Entrepreneurship, 2007). *Dissertation Abstracts International, 68 (05).* (UMI No. 3268676).

Chen, Y., Gupta, A., & Hoshower, L. (2006). Factors that motivate business faculty to conduct research. *Journal of Education for Business, 81 (4)*, 179-189.

Chiu, W., Chan, A., Snape, E., & Redman, T. (2001). Age stereotypes and discriminatory attitudes toward older workers: An east-west comparison. *Human Relations, 54 (5)*, 629-661.

College and University Professional Association for Human Resource –CUPA-HR (2006). Think tank report on the future of higher education. Retrieved August 1, 2007, from http://www.cupahr.org.knowledgecenter

Collins, J. F. (1982, December). How to motivate your employees. *Nation's Business,* 48.

Comm, C. L., & Mathaisel, D. F. X. (2003). A case study of the implications of faculty workload and compensation for improving academic quality. *The International Journal of Educational Management, 17 (4/5)*, 200-210.

Cook, J. D., Hepworth, S. J., Wall, T. D., & Warr, P. B. (1981). *The experience of work: A compendium and review of 249 measures and their use.* London: Academic Press.

Couper, M. P. (2000). Web surveys: A review of issues and approaches. *Public Opinion Quarterly, 64*, 464-494.

Cowherd, D. M., & Levine, D. J. (1992). Product quality and pay equity between lower-level employees and top management: An investigation of distributive justice theory. *Administrative Science Quarterly, 37*, 302-320.

Cranny, C. J., Smith, P.C., & Stone, E. F. (1992). *Job Satisfaction.* New York: Lexington Books.

Crosby, F. (1976). A model of egoistical relative deprivation. *Psychological Review*, *83*, 95-113

Crow, S. M., & Hartman, S. J. (1995). Can't get no satisfaction. *Leadership & Organization Development Journal*, *16*, 34-38.

Cummings, T. G., & Bigelow, J. (1976). Satisfaction, job involvement and intrinsic motivation: An extension of Lawler and Hall's factor analysis. *Journal of Applied Psychology, 61,* 523-525.

Currall, S. C., Towler, A. J., Judge, T. A., & Kohn, L. (2005). Pay satisfaction and organizational outcomes. *Personnel Psychology*, *58*, 613-641.

Curtis, J.W. (2005). Inequities persist for women and non-tenure-track faculty: The annual report on the economic status of the profession 2004-05. *Academe, 91 (2)*, 21-29.

Datamonitor (2005, May). Global education services: Industry profile. Retrieved August 11, 2007 from www.datamonitor.com.

Day, T. A. (2005). Substitutes for job satisfaction: Family-supportive programs (Doctoral Dissertation, Nova Southeastern University – Huizenga Graduate School of Business and Entrepreneurship, 2005). *Dissertation Abstracts International, 66 (12)*. (UMI No.3197580).

Deci, E. L. (1972). The effect of contingent and noncontingent rewards and controls on intrinsic motivation. *Organizational Behavior and Human Performance*, *8*, 217-229.

Deutskens, E., Ruyter, K.D., & Wetzels. (2006). An assessment of equivalence between online mail surveys in service research. *Journal of Service Research, 8 (4)*, 346-355.

Deutsch, M. (1985). *Distributive justice: A social psychological perspective*. New Haven, CT: Yale University Press.

Dictionary of Human Resources & Personnel Management, *Peter Collin Publishing* (1997). Retrieved 08 October 2006, from xreferplus. http://0-www.xreferplus.com.novacat.nova.edu:80/entry/868570

Dunford, B., Boudreau, J., & Boswell, W. (2005). Out-of-the-money: The impact of underwater stock options on executive job search. *Personnel Psychology, 58 (1)*, 67-101.

Ehrenberg, R.G., & Zhang, L. (2005). Do tenured and tenure-track faculty matter? *The Journal of Human Resources, 40 (3)*, 647-659.

Einstein, W. O. (n.d.). Preparing a survey research paper. Charlton College of Business. University of Massachusetts Dartmouth.

Evans, J. R., & Mathur, A. (2005). The value of online surveys. *Internet Research, 15 (2)*, 195-219.

Falcone, P. (2006, March). Preserving restless top performers. *HR Magazine, 51(3)*, 117-122.

Flanagan, R. J., Strauss, G & Ulman, L. (1974). Worker discontent and work place behavior. *Industrial Relations*, *13*, 101-23.

Fogg, P. (2006). Young Ph.D.'s say collegiality matters more than salary. *The Chronicle of Higher Education, 53 (6)*, A1.

Frick, B., Prinz, J., & Winkelmann, K. (2003). Pay inequalities and team performance: Empirical evidence from the North American major leagues. *International Journal of Manpower, 24,* 472 - 491.

Fricker, R. D. & Schonlau, M. (2002). Advantages and disadvantage of internet research surveys: Evidence from the literature. *Field Methods, 14 (4),* 347-367.

Fricker, S., Galesic, M., Tourangeau, R., & Yan, T. (2005). An experimental comparison of web and telephone surveys. *Public Opinion Quarterly, 69 (3),* 370-392.

Furnham, A. (2005). Paying for performance. *European Business Forum, 20,* 16-18.

Furnham, A. (2006). Pouring money down the drain? *The British Journal of Administrative Management,* 26 -28.

Furnham, A., & Argyle, M. (1998). *The psychology of money.* London: Routledge.

Furnham, A., & Okamura, R. (1999). Your money or your life: Behavioral and emotional predictors of money pathology. *Human Relations, 52 (9),* 1157-1177.

Gardner, D. G., Dyne, L.V., & Pierce, J. L. (2004). The effects of pay level on organization-based self-esteem and performance: A field study. *Journal of Occupational and Organizational Psychology, 77,* 307-323.

Gardner, T. (1999). When pay for performance works too well: The negative impact of pay dispersion. *The Academy of Management Executive, 13,* 101 - 103.

Garland, H. (1973). Effects of piece rate underpayment and overpayments on job performance: A test equity theory with a new induction procedure. *Journal of Applied Social Psychology, 57,* 325-334.

Gerhart, B. (1987). How important are dispositional factors as determinants of job satisfaction? Implications for job design and other personnel programs. *Journal of Applied Social Psychology,* 366-373.

Gerhart, B., & Milkovich, G. T. (1992). Employee compensation: Research and practice. In M.D. Dunnette & L.M. Hough (Eds.), *Handbook of Industrial and Organizational Psychology, 3,* 481-570.

Gerhart, B., Minkoff, H. B., & Olsen, R. N. (1995). Employee compensation: Theory, practice, and evidence: Handbook of Human Resource Management. Cambridge: Blackwell.

Gilmore, D. C., Beehr, T.A., & Richter, D. J. (1979). Effects of leader behaviors on subordinate performance and satisfaction: A laboratory experiment with student employees. *Journal of Applied Psychology, 64 (1).* 166-172.

Gini, A. (2000). My Job My Self: Work and the Creation f the Modern Individual, New York: Routledge.

Gneezy, U., & Rustichini, A. (2000). Pay enough or don't pay at all. *Quarterly Journal of Economics, 115,* 791-810.

Goldberg, H., & Lewis, R. T. (1978). Money madness: The psychology of saving, spending, loving and hating money. London: Springwood.

Goltz, S. (2005). Women's appeals for equity at American universities. *Human Relations, 58 (6),* 763-797.

Gomez-Mejia, L. R. (1984). Faculty satisfaction with pay and other job dimensions under union and nonunion conditions. *Academy of Management Journal, Sep,* 591-602.

Gravois, J. (2007). Alleging gender bias, 8 professors sue Penn State. *The Chronicle of Higher Education, 53 (36),* A23.

Granello, D. H., & Wheaton, J. E. (2004). Online data collection: Strategies for research. *Journal of Counseling and Development, 82 (4),* 387-393.

Greenberg, J., & Leventhal, G. S. (1976). Equity and the use of over-rewarded to motivate performance. *Journal of Personality and Social Psychology, 34,* 179-190.

Greenberg, J. (1987). Reactions to procedural injustice in payment distribution: Do the means justify the ends? *Journal of Applied Psychology, 72,* 55-61.

Greenberg, J. (1990). Employee theft as a reaction to underpayment of inequity: The hidden cost of pay cuts. *Journal of Applied Psychology, 75,* 561-568.

Griffin, R. W. (1990). *Management.* Texas: Houghton Mifflin Company.

Gray, J., & Chapman, R. (1999). Conflicting signals: The labor market for college-educated workers. *Journal of Economic Issues, 33 (3),* 661-676.

Guzzo, R. A., & Katzell, R. A. (1987). *Effects of economic incentives on productivity: A psychological view.* Totowa, NJ: Rowman and Littlefield.

Hackman, J. R., & Lawler, E. E. (1971). Employee reaction to job characteristics. *Journal of Applied Psychology, 55,* 259-286.

Hackman, J. R., & Oldham, G. R. (1975). Development of the job diagnostic survey. *Journal of Applied Psychology, 60,* 159-170.

Hackman, J. R., & Oldham, G. R. (1976). Motivation through the design of work: Test of a theory. *Organizational Behavior and Human Performance, 16,* 250-279.

Hackman, J. R., & Oldham, G. R. (1980). *Work redesign.* Reading, MA: Addison Wesley.

Hair, J. F., Anderson, R. E., Tatham, R .L., & Black, W. C. (1998). *Multivariate data analysis.* New Jersey: Prentice Hall.

Harde', P. L., Xie, K., & Ly, C. (2005). Production and data management issues for digital questionnaire administration. *Performance Improvement (May/June),* 44 (5). 33-40.

Hastings, R. R. (2007, May). Women encounter obstacles, attitudes on the way to the top. *HR Magazine, 52 (5).* Retrieved August 11, 2007, from http://www.shrm.org/diversity/07May.

Hechler, P. D., & Wiener, Y. (1974). Chronic self-esteem as a moderator of performance consequences of pay. *Organizational Behavior and Human Performance, 11,* 97-105.

Hellerman, M., Kochanski, J., Adwin, J., & Wong, C. (2007, April). Making merit pay matter. *HR Magazine, 52 (4).* Retrieved August 11, 2007, from http://www.shrm.org/rewards/07April.

Hemmasi, M., Graf, L. A., & Lust, J. A. (1992). Correlates of pay and benefit satisfaction: The unique case of public university faculty. *Public Personnel Management, 21,* 429-441.

Heneman, H. G., & Judge, T. A., (2000). *Compensation attitudes*. San Francisco: Jossey-Bass.

Herzberg, F. (1968). One more time: Howe do you motivate employees? *Harvard Business Review, 48,* 53-62.

Herzberg, F., Mausner, B., & Snyderman, B. (1959). *The motivation to work*. New York: John Wiley & Sons.

Hickok, E. (2006). Higher education needs reform, too. *The Chronicle of Higher Education, 52 (27),* B48.

Hinrichs, J. R. (1969). Correlation of employee evaluation of pay increases. *Journal of Applied Psychology, 53,* 481-489.

Hoover's Custom Report Builder (2007 August). Retrieved August 1, 2007 available from http://www.hoovers.com.

Horowitz, A. (2004). Zooming in on customers. *Sales and Marketing Management, 156, (11).* 21.

Howard, N. H. (1982). Job Involvement among managers and its relationship to demographic, psychological, and situational forces (Doctoral Dissertation - Stevens Institute of Technology, March 1984). *Dissertation Abstracts International, 44 (09).* UMI No. 8323094.

Huseman, R. C., & Hatfield, J. D. (1990). Equity theory and the managerial matrix. *Training & Development Journal,* 98-102.

Jaques, E. (1961). *Equitable payment*. New York: Wiley.

Jenkins, G. D., Mitra, A., Gupta, N., & Shaw, J. D. (1998). Are financial incentives related to performance? A meta-analytic review of empirical research. *Journal of Applied Psychology, 83,* 777-787.

Jones, A. P., James, L.R., & Bruni, J. R. (1975). Perceived leadership behavior and employee confidence in the leader as moderated by job involvement. *Journal of Applied Psychology, 60,* 146-149.

Kaiser, H. F. (1970). A second –generation little jiffy. *Psychometrika, 35,* 401-415.

Kaiser, H. F. (1974). Little jiffy, Mark IV. *Educational and Psychometrika, 35,* 111-117.

Kasten, K. L. (1984). Tenure and merit pay as rewards for research, teaching and service at a research university. *Journal of Higher Education, 55,* 500-514.

Kauffman, N. (1987). Motivating the older worker. *Sam Advanced Management Journal, 52 (2),* 43-48.

Kauhanen, A., & Piekkola, H. (2006). What makes performance-related pay schemes work? Finish evidence. *Journal of Management Governance, 10,* 149-177.

Kelloway, K. E., Catano, V. M., & Carroll, A. E. (2000). Psychological involvement in the union. *Canadian Journal of Behavioural Science, 32 (3),* 163-167.

Kerber, L. K. (2005). We must make the academic workplace more humane and equitable. *The Chronicle of Higher Education, 51 (28),* B6.

Kim, J., & Garman, T. (2004). Financial stress, pay satisfaction and workplace performance. *Compensation and Benefits Review,* 69-76.

Kim, J. S. & Schuler, R.S. (1979). The nature of the task as a moderator of the relationship between extrinsic feedback and employee responses. *Academy of Management Journal, 22,* 157-162.

Kinnoin, C. M. (2005). An examination of the relationship between family-friendly policies and employee job satisfaction, intent to leave, and organizational commitment (Doctoral dissertation, Nova Southeastern University – Huizenga Graduate School of Business and Entrepreneurship, 2005). *Dissertation Abstracts International, 66 (06).* (UMI No.3180657).

Kinser, K., & Levy, D. C. (2005, February). The for-profit sector: U.S. patterns and international echoes in higher education. *Program for Research on Private Higher Education* (WP No. 5). Albany, New York.

Kirkcaldy, B., & Furnham, A. (1993). Predictors of beliefs about money. *Psychological Reports, 73,* 1079-1082.

Kovach, K. A. (1987). What motivates employees? Workers and supervisors give different answers. *Business Horizons, 30,* 58-65.

Kratz, R. D., & Mets, B. (2005). Finding an incentive plan that actually works. *Physician Executive, 31 (3),* 54-56.

Kreps, D. M. (1997). Intrinsic motivation and extrinsic incentives. *The American Economic Review, 87,* 359.

Kuhnert, K. W., & Palmer, D. R. (1991). Job security, health, and the intrinsic and extrinsic characteristics of work. *Group & Organization Studies, 16 (2),* 178-192.

Landstrom, R.H. (1998). Career women in their first pregnancy: How expectations of career-motherhood conflicts relate to psychological distress (Doctoral Dissertation, Adelphi University – The Gordon F. Derner Institute of Advanced Psychological Studies, June 1998). *Dissertation Abstracts International, 58 (12).* (UMI No.9820647).

Lawler, E. E., & Porter, L. W. (1967). The effect of performance on job satisfaction. *Industrial relations, 7,* 20-28.

Lawler, E.E., & Hall, D. T. (1970). Relationship of job characteristics to job involvement, satisfaction and intrinsic motivation. *Journal of Applied Psychology, 54,* 305-312.

Lawler, E. E. (1971). Pay and organizational effectiveness: A psychological view. New York: McGraw-Hill.

Lawler, E. E., & Worley, C. G. (2006 March/April) Winning support for organizational change: Designing employee reward systems that keep on working. *Ivey Business Journal,* 1-5.

Lawler, E. E. (1981). *Pay and organization development.* Reading, MA: Addison-Wesley.

Lenhart, N. A. (2006). How much will employee financial stress cost your company in 2006? *Employee Benefit Plan Review, 22 (2),* 13-15.

Leslie, D. W. (1998). Redefining tenure: Tradition versus the new political economy of higher education. *The American Behavioral Scientist, 41 (5),* 652-680.

Likert, R. (1967). The human organization: Its management and value. New York: McGraw-Hill.

Llorente, M, R., & Macias, F, E., (2005). Job satisfaction as an indicator of the quality of work. *Journal of Socio-Economics, 34,* 656-673.

Locke, E. A. (1969). What is job satisfaction? *Organizational Behavior and Human Performance, 4,* 309-336.

Lodahl, T., & Kejner, M. (1965). The definition and measurement of job involvement. *Journal of Applied Psychology, 49,* 24-33.

Longmate, J. & Cosco, F. (2002). Part-time instructors deserve equal pay for equal work. *The Chronicle of Higher Education, 48 (34),* B.14.

Loury, D. L. (1997). The gender earning gap among college-educated workers. *Industrial & Labor relations Review, 50 (4),* 580-594.

.Magnusen, A. (1987). Faculty evaluation, performance and pay. *Journal of Higher Education, 58,* 516-529.

Malhotra, N. K. (2007). *Marketing research an applied orientation.* Upper Saddle River, NJ: Pearson Prentice Hall.

Marchant, G. J., & Newman, I. (1994). Faculty activities and rewards: Views from education administrators in the USA. *Assessment & Evaluation in Higher Education, 19,* 144-152.

Mason, E. S. (1995). Gender differences in job satisfaction. *The Journal of Social Psychology, 135,* 143 - 149.

Mathis, R. L., & Jackson, J. H. (2000). *Human Resource Management.* United States: South-Western College Publishing.

Mawhinney, T., & Gowen, C. (1990). Gainsharing and the law of effect as the matching law: A theoretical framework. *Journal of Organizational Behavior Management, 11,* 61-75.

McAfee, R. B., & Glassman, M. (2005). The case against pay inversion. *Sam Advance Management Journal, 70 (3),* 24-29.

McClelland, D. C., Atkinson, J. W., Clark, R. A., & Lowell, E. L. (1953). *The Achievement Motive.* New York: Appleton - Century - Crofts.

McConnell, C. A. (1992). The relationship between job involvement and frequency of absence among registered nurses practicing in an acute care hospital (Doctoral Dissertation, University of Florida – College of Nursing, Summer 1993). *Dissertation Abstracts International, 31 (02).* (UMI No.1350431).

McDowell, W. C., Boyd, N. G., & Bowler, W. M. (2007). Overreward and the impostor phenomenon. *Journal of Managerial Issues, 19 (1),* 95-110.

McEvoy, G. M, & Cascio, W. F. (1989). Cumulative evidence of the relationship between employee age and job performance. *Journal of Applied Psychology, 74 (1),* 11-17.

McEwen, T. (1988). The impact of type and level of college degree on managerial communication competence. *Journal of Education for Business, 73 (6),* 352-358.

McFillen, J. M., & Podsakoff, P. M. (1983). A coordinated approach to motivation can increase productivity. *Personnel Administrator, 29,* 45-53.

Medina, J., Saegert, J., & Gresham, A. (1996). Comparison of Mexican-American and Anglo-American attitudes to money. *Journal of Consumer Affairs, 30,* 124-145.

Merriman, K. (2005). Avoiding the performance pay employee entitlement trap. *Workspan, 48,* 64-68.

Merriam-Webster Online Dictionary, Retrieved April 10, 2006. from http:// www.m-w.com.

Milbourn, G., & Haight, T. (2004). Teaching the job satisfaction audit project to business school students. *Journal of American Academy of Business*, 5, 353-356.

Milkovich, G. T., & Newman, J. M. (1993). *Compensation*. Homewood, IL: Irwin.

Miller, G. A. (1967). Professionals in bureaucracy: Alienation among industrial scientists and engineers. *American Sociological Review*, 32, 755-768.

Millman, S. (2007). For the first time in 3 years faculty salaries beat inflation. *The Chronicle of Higher Education, 53 (33)*, 10.

Mitchell, T. R., & Mickel, A. E. (1999). The meaning of money: An individual - difference perspective. *Academy of Management Review*, 3, 568-578.

Monks, J. (2007). The relative earnings of contingent faculty in higher education. *Journal of Labor Research, 28 (3)*, 487-507.

Morris, J. H., & Snyder, R. A. (1979). A second look at need for achievement and need for autonomy as moderators of role perception-role outcome relationships. *Journal of Applied Psychology, 64,* 173-178.

Morrison, R. (2004). Informal relationships in the workplace: Associations with job satisfaction, organisational commitment and turnover intentions. *New Zealand Journal of Psychology, 33*, 114-129.

Morse, N. C. (1953). *Satisfaction in the white-collar job. Survey Research Center*. Ann Arbor, MI: University of Michigan.

Nelson, C. (1997). Superstars. *Academe*, Jan-Feb, 38-54.

Nelson, N. C. (2006). Valuing employees: Employees are eager to work hard, but managers need to listen to their needs. *HR Magazine, 51 (2)*, 117-122.

Okpara, J. O., Squillace, M., & Erondu, E. A. (2004). Gender differences and job satisfaction: A study of university teachers in United States. *Women in Management Review, 20*, 177-190.

Oldham, G. R. (1976). Job characteristics and internal motivation: The moderating effect of interpersonal and individual variables. *Human Relations*, 29, 559-569.

O'Reilly, C. A., III & Pfeffer, J. (2000). Hidden Value: How Great Companies Achieve Extraordinary Results with Ordinary People. Boston: Harvard Business School Press.

Oshagbemi, T. (1995). Job satisfaction of workers in higher education. *Reflections on Higher Education, 7*, 65-89.

Oshagbemi, T. (1996). Job satisfaction of UK academics. *Educational Management and Administration, 24*, 389-400.

Oshagbemi, T. (2000a). Correlates of pay satisfaction in higher education. *The International Journal of Educational Management Bradford*, 14, 31-39.

Oshagbemi, T. (2000b). Gender differences in the job satisfaction of university teachers. *Women in Management Review, 15,* 331 - 142.

Oshagbemi, T., & Hickson, C. (2003). Some aspects of overall satisfaction: A binomial logit model. *Journal of Managerial Psychology, 18 (4)*, 357-367.

Parsons, T. (1967). *Sociological Theory and Modern Society*. New York: Free Press.

Peiperl, M., & Jones, B. (2001). Workaholics and overworkers: Productivity or pathology. *Group & Organization Management, 26*, 369.

Perry, J. L., Mesch, D., & Paarlberg C. (2006). Motivating employees in a new governance era: The performance paradigm revisited. *Public Administration Review, 66 (4)*, 505-514.

Petrimoulx, S. (2007, January). The problem with pay-for-performance plans (and what to do about them. *SHRM Online*. Retrieved August 11, 2007, from http://www.shrm.org/rewards/library_published/compensation/nonIC/CMS_ 019977.asp.

Pfeffer, J. (1998). Harvard Business Review on Managing People. *Six dangerous myths about pay*. Boston: MA: Harvard Business School Press.

Pfeffer, J. & Langton, N. (1993). The effect of wage dispersion on satisfaction, productivity, and working collaboratively: evidence from college and university faculty. *Administrative Science Quarterly, 38*, 382-407.

Piamonte, John S. (1979). In praise of monetary motivation. *Personnel Journal, 58*, 597.

Porter, L. W. (1962). Job attitudes in management: Perceived deficiencies in need fulfillment as a function of job level. *Journal of Applied Psychology, 46*, 375-384.

Porter, L. W., & Smith, F. J. (1970). *The Etiology of Organizational Commitment* (Unpublished paper). Irvine, CA: University of California.

Quinn, R. P., & Staines, G. L. (1979). *The 1977 Quality of Employment Survey*. Ann Arbor, Michigan: University of Michigan.

Rainey, A. (2006). Share of students in the science shrinks. *The Chronicle of Higher Education, 52 (36)*, A35.

Ramsey, R., Lassk, F.G., & Marshall, G. W. (1995). A critical evaluation of a measure of job involvement: The use of the Lodahl and Kejner (1965) scale with salespeople. *The Journal of Personal Selling & Sales Management, 15* (3), 65-75.

Renier, J. J. (1983). Productivity and personal objective setting. *Resource* (August), 6.

Roethlisberger, F. J., Dickson, W. J., & Wright, H. R. (1956). *Management and the Worker*. Massachusetts: Harvard University Press.

Rhoades, L., & Eisenberger, R. (2002). Perceived organizational support: A review of the literature. *Journal of Applied Psychology, 87*, 698-714.

Robbins, S. P. (2000). *Organizational Behavior*. New Jersey: Prentice Hall.

Ross, I. C., Zander, A. (1957). Need Satisfaction and employee turnover. *Personnel Psychology, 10*, 327-338.

Rubery, J., Earnshaw, J., Marchington, M., Cooke, F. L., & Vincent, S. (2002). Changing organizational forms and the employment relationship. *Journal of Management Studies, 39 (5)*, 645-672.

Russell, B. (1930). *The Conquest of Happiness*. New York: Liveright.

Rynes, S. L., Gerhart, B., & Minette, K. A. (2004). The importance of pay in employee motivation: Discrepancies between what people say and what they do. *Human Resource Management, 43*, 381-394.

Saari, L. M., & Judge, T. A. (2004). Employee attitudes and job satisfaction. *Human Resource Management, 43 (4)*, 395-407.

Sak, A. M., & Waldman, D. A. (1998). The relationship between age and job performance evaluations for entry-level professionals. *Journal of Organizational Behavior, 19 (4)*, 409-419.

Samad, S. (2005). Unraveling the organizational commitment and job performance relationship: Exploring the moderating effect of job satisfaction. *The Business Review, 4 (2)*, 79-84.

Sammer, J. (2007, June). Weighing pay incentives. *HR Magazine, 52 (6)*, 65-68.

Saucer, W. I., & York, C. M. (1978). Sex differences in job satisfaction: A re-examination. *Personnel Psychology, 31*, 537-547.

Schaffer, R. H. (1953). Job satisfaction as related to need satisfaction in work. *Psychological Monographs, 67*, 14.

Schulz, E. R., & Tanguay, D. M. (2006). Merit pay in a public higher education institution: Questions of impact and attitudes. *Public Personnel Management, 35*, 71-87.

Seashore, S. E., Lawler, E. E., Mirvis, P., & Cammann, C. (1982). *Observing and Measuring Organizational Change: A Guide to Field Practice*. New York: Wiley.

Seeman, M. (1959). On the meaning of alienation. *American Sociological Review, 24*, 783-791.

Seery, B. M. (1990). Generalized and specific sources of job satisfaction related to attrition and retention of teachers of behavior-disordered and severely emotionally disturbed students in Georgia (Doctoral dissertation, Georgia State University – College of Education, 1990). *Dissertation Abstracts International, 51 (12)*, 4089. (UMI No.9112211).

Shapiro, J. (2001). Winning tenure, losing the thrill. *The Chronicle of Higher Education, 48 (12)*, B7.

Shauman, K. A. (2006). Occupational sex segregation and the earnings of occupations: What causes the link among college-educated workers? *Social Science Research, 35 (3)*, 577-620.

Shaw, J. D., Gupta, N., & Delery, J. E. (2002). Pay dispersion and workforce performance: Moderating effects of incentives and interdependence. *Strategic Management Journal, 23*, 491 - 507.

Sheehan, B. & McMillan, S. J. (1999). Response variation in e-mail surveys: An exploration. *Journal of Advertising Research, 39 (4)*, 45-57.

SHRM Workplace Trends Program (2006, December). Wage gap remains. *HR Magazine, 51 (12)*. Retrieved August 11, 2007, from http://www.shrm.org/trends/o6December.

Siggins, J. A. (1993). Job satisfaction and performance in a changing environment. *Library Trends, 41*, 299-315.

Sims, R. L. (2000). *Bivariate data analysis: A practical guide*. New York, NY. Nova Science Publishers, Inc.

Singh, D., Fujita, F., & Norton, D. S. (2004). Determinants of satisfaction with pay among nursing home administrators. *Journal of American Academy of Business, 5* (1/2), 230-236.

Smith, P.C., Kendall, L.M., & Hulin, C. L. (1969). *The Measurement of Satisfaction in Work and Retirement*. Chicago; Rand McNally.

Staw, B. M., & Ross, J. (1985). Stability in the midst of change a dispositional approach to job attitudes. *Journal of Applied Psychology, 70*, 469-481.

Staw, B. M., Bell, N. E., & Clausen, J. A. (1986). The depositional approach to job attitudes: A lifetime longitudinal test. *Administrative Science Quarterly, 31*, 56-77.

Stiffler, M. A. (2006a). Incentive compensation management: Making pay-for-performance a reality. *Performance Improvement, 45 (1)*, 25-31.

Stiffler, M. A. (2006b). Move from managing to driving performance. *Performance Improvement, 45 (9)*, 17-19.

Stockman, K. (2006, February 20). Enrollment growing at for-profit college: Proprietary schools focus on getting students into the workforce. *The Journal Gazette*. Retrieved August 22, 2007, from: http://www.southbendtribune.com/apps/pbcs.dll/article?AID=/20060220/News01/6022003

Sturman, M., C., Cheramie, R, A., & Cashen, L, H. (2002). How to compare apples to oranges: Balancing internal candidates' job-performance data with external candidates' selection-test results. *Cornell Hotel and Restaurant Administration Quarterly, 43*, 27-41.

Sturman, M. C., Trevor, C. O., Boudreau, J. W., & Gerhart, B. (2003). Is it worth it to win the talent war? Evaluating the utility of performance-based pay. *Personnel Psychology, 56*, 997–1018.

Summer, T. P., & Hendrix, W. P. (1991). Modeling the role of pay equity perceptions: A field study. *Journal of Occupational Psychology, 64*, 145-155.

Sweeney, P. D., & McFarlin, D.B. (2005). Wage comparisons with similar and dissimilar. *Journal of Occupational and Organizational Psychology, 78*, 113-131.

Tang, T. L. P. (1992). The meaning of money revisited. *Journal of Organizational Behavior, 13*, 197-202.

Tang, T. L. P. (1995). The development of a short money ethic scale: Attitudes toward money and pay satisfaction revisited. *Personal Individual Differences, 6*, 809-816.

Tang, T.L.P. (2007). Income and quality of life: Does the love of money make a difference? *Journal of Business Ethics, 72 (4)*, 375-394.

Tang, T. L. P., & Talpade, M (1999). Sex differences in satisfaction with pay and co-workers: faculty and staff at a public institution of higher education. *Public Personnel Management, 28*, 345-350.

Tang, T. L. P., Kim, J. K., & Tang, T. L. (2002). Endorsement of the money ethic, income, and life satisfaction: A comparison of full-time employees, part-time employees, and non-employed university students. *Journal of Managerial Psychology, 17 (6)*, 442-468.

Tang, T. L. P., & Chiu, R. K. (2003). Income, money ethic, pay satisfaction, commitment, and unethical behavior: Is the love of money the root of evil for Hong Kong employees? *Journal of Business Ethics, 46 (1)*, 13-30.

Tang, T. L. P, Luna-Arocas, R., Sutarso, T., & Tang, D.S. H. (2004). Does the love of money moderate and mediate the income-pay satisfaction relationship? *Journal of Managerial Psychology, 19*, 111- 120.

Tang, T. L. P. (2006). Income and quality of life: Does the love of money make a difference? *Journal of Business Ethics, 72 (4),* 375-394.

Tang, T. L. P., Tang, T. L. N., & Homaifar, B. Y. (2006). Income, the love of money, pay comparison, and pay satisfaction: Race and gender as moderators. *Journal of Managerial Psychology, 21 (5)*, 476-491.

Taynor, J., & Deaux, K. (1973). When women are more deserving than men; Equity, attribution, and perceived sex differences. *Journal of Personality and Social Psychology, 28*, 360-367.

Taynor, J., & Deaux, K. (1975). Equity and perceived sex differences; Role behavior as defined by the task, mode, and the actor. *Journal of Personality and Social Psychology, 32*, 381-390.

Teach, E. (2006, December). A productive debate: Is the link between pay and productivity broken? *CFO, 22 (13)*, 31-32.

Terpstra, D. E., & Honoree, A. L. (2005). Employees' responses to merit pay inequity. *Compensation and Benefits Review, 37*, 51-57.

Thompson, A. (1980). How to motivate. *Management Today*, 111.

Thozhur, S. M., Riley, M., & Szivas, E. (2006). Money attitudes and pay satisfaction of the low paid. *Journal of Managerial Psychology, 21*, 163-172.

Trahant, B. (2007). Debunking five myths concerning employee engagement. *Public Manager, 36 (1)*, 53-59.

Trank, C. Q., Rynes, S. L., & Bretz, R. D. (2002). Attracting applicants in the war for talent: Differences in work preferences among high achievers. *Journal of Business and Psychology, 16*, 331 - 345.

Truby, K. (2003). Short-order teachers: The joys and frustrations of the university lecturer. *ADFL Bulletin, 34*, 42-44.

Truxillo, D. M., Bennett, S. R., & Collins, M. L. (1998). College education and police job performance: A ten-year study. *Public Personnel Management, 27 (2)*, 269-281.

Tu, L., Plaisent, M., Bernard, P., & Maguiraga, L. (2005). Comparative age differences of job satisfaction on faculty at higher education level. *The International Journal of Educational Management, 19 (2/3)*, 259-267.

Udechukwu, I. (2007). The influence of intrinsic and extrinsic satisfaction on organizational exit (voluntary turnover): Evidence from a correctional setting. *Journal of Applied Management and Entrepreneurship, 12 (1)*, 127-142.

Viswesvaran, C., & Ones, D. S. (2000). Perspectives on model of job performance. *International Journal of Selection and Assessment, 8 (4)*, 216-226.

Vitell, S. J., Paolillo, J. G. P., & Singh, J. J. (2006). The role of money and religiosity in determining consumers' ethical beliefs. *Journal of Business Ethics, 64*, 117-124.

Vroom, V. H. (1964). *Work and motivation.* New York: John Wiley & Son.

Vroom, V. H. (1982). *Work and motivation.* New York: Robert E. Krieger Publishing Company & Son.

Vroom, V. H. (1995). *Work and motivation.* San Francisco, CA: Jossey-Bass.

Wahba, M. A. (1971). Equity theory as a predictor of payoff apportionment among partners in coalition formations. *Psychonomic Science, 24,* 177-180.

Waldman, D. A., & Avolio, B. J. (1986). A meta-analysis of age differences in job performance. Journal of Applied Psychology, 71 (1), 33-38.

Ward, D. (2006). Master of all whom you survey. *PRweek (U.S. Ed.), 9* (38), 22- 35.

Wasley, P. (2007). Gender gap in pay widens over time. *The Chronicle of Higher Education, 53 (35),* A21.

Weiss, D. J., Dawis, R. V., England, G.W. and Lofquist, L. H. (1967). *Manual for the Minnesota Satisfaction Questionnaire.* Industrial Relations Center, University of Minnesota.

Wessler, R. L. (1984). The psychology of motivation. *Marketing Communication* (May), 29-32.

White, M., & Mackenzie-Davey, K. (2003). Feeling valued at work? A qualitative study of corporate training consultants. *Career Development International, 8,* 228-235.

Williams, W. M., & Ceci, S. J. (2007). Does tenure really work? *The Chronicle of Higher Education, 53 (27),* B16.

Wilson, R. (2004). Where the elite teach it's still a man's world. *The Chronicle of Higher Education, 51 (15),* A8.

Wilson, R. (1998). For some adjunct faculty members, the tenure track holds little appeal. *The Chronicle of Higher Education, 44 (46),* A8.

Wise, D.A. (1975). Academic achievement and job performance. *The American Economic Review, 65 (3),* 350-366.

Wood, J. (2006). Opportunity, ease, encouragement, and shame: A short course in pitching for-profit education. *The Chronicle of Higher Education, 52 (19),* B10.

Young, I. P. (1997). Dimensions of employee compensation: Practical and theoretical implications for superintendents. *Educational Administration Quarterly, 33,* 506-525.

VII - Index

Expectancy Theory · 4, 31
extrinsic rewards · 9, 10, 17, 18, 31
Extrinsic Rewards · 5, 17, 31

A

age · 7, 6, 10, 12, 13, 15, 28, 32, 35, 38, 42, 46, 47, 51, 52, 53, 62, 65, 66, 67, 68, 69, 71, 72, 81, 84, 86, 87
American Association of University · 14, 15
American InterContinental University · 2
Americans · 18
Attitudes toward money · 72, 85

B

Beta coefficients · 52, 53, 54, 55, 56, 57, 59, 60, 68

C

Chapter five · 5
Chapter four · 5
Chapter one · 5
Chapter three · 5
Chapter two · 5
college education · 16
Comparisons · 65
Convenience sampling · 45
copyright · 2

D

data analysis · 5, 29, 44, 70, 78, 84
data collection procedure · 5, 29, 44
demographics · 45, 63
departmental climate · 15
dependent variables · 31, 52, 68, 69
descriptive frequencies · 45, 63
DeVry University · 2

E

Economic Status of the Profession · 13
education industry · 1
Empirical data · 13
Employees · 12, 19, 21, 24, 25, 28, 72, 82, 86
Equity theory · 16, 79, 87

F

factor analysis · 45, 49, 63, 76
financial stress · 17, 18, 28, 80
Florida · 1
For-Profit Education Industry · 2
For-Profit Institution · 4, 32
for-profit institutions · 7, 3, 4, 5, 6, 7, 9, 29, 30, 32, 38, 39, 40, 44, 45, 51, 52, 53, 54, 55, 56, 57, 58, 59, 60, 61, 62, 65, 67, 68, 69, 70, 72

G

Gender · 5, 10, 13, 40, 42, 48, 51, 54, 55, 56, 81, 82, 87
General Linear Model Univariate · 52, 54, 55, 56, 57, 60

H

high achievers · 24, 25, 86
Higher Education · 1, 2, 15, 66, 73, 74, 76, 78, 79, 80, 81, 82, 83, 84, 87
Higher pay levels · 3, 20
HR Practitioners · 7, 69, 70, 71, 72
Human Resource · 7, 2, 69, 72, 75, 77, 81, 83
Hypothesis Model Summary · 40

I

independent variable · 31, 32, 51, 60, 68
intrinsic motivation · 17, 18, 76, 80

J

Job Involvement Scale · 3, 4, 31, 33, 34, 36, 37, 39, 40, 41, 44, 49, 50, 51, 65, 68
job performance · 7, 3, 5, 6, 7, 9, 10, 12, 13, 15, 17, 20, 21, 22, 24, 28, 29, 31, 32, 33, 37, 38, 39, 41, 43, 44, 45, 51, 52, 53, 54, 56, 58, 59,

Author Biography

Dr. Joann Adeogun, PHR, is the principal owner of Adeogun & Associates, LLC an HR Consulting Company that specializes in process improvements using a variety of methods to attract, retain and motivate employees. She is also an adjunct instructor at several universities specializing in Human Resources Management for graduate and undergraduate students. Joann has worked as a Director of Compliance, Director of Institutional Effectiveness, Portal Coordinator, Trainer and Instructor. She is a contributor to the Atlanta Journal Constitution (AJC) column "Ask HR" and on the Business Program Advisory Committee of Herzing College Online Business and Human Resources Programs. Most recently she has been invited to become a member of the Commission's Peer Review Corps for The Higher Learning Commission, NCA, Academic Quality Improvement Program.

Joann received her terminal degree from Nova Southern University, H. Wayne Huizenga School of Business in Business Administration specializing in Human Resources Management, graduate degree from Troy College specializing in Human Resources Management and undergraduate degree from Shorter College in Business Management. She is a certified Professional in Human Resources Management (PHR) and a member of SHRM National, SHRM Atlanta and CUPA-HR. Joann is a contributor to the book *"Earning a Doctorate Degree in the 21ˢᵗ Century: Challenges and Joys."* She has also published in the Journal of Applied Management and Entrepreneurship, the Journal of Applied Business Research, and The eHuman Resources (SHRM Atlanta Chapter). Joann can be emailed at dradeogun@comcast.net, adeogunassociates@comcast.net or adeogun@nova.edu.

www.ingramcontent.com/pod-product-compliance
Lightning Source LLC
Chambersburg PA
CBHW032106080426
42733CB00006B/438